INHALE

Breathe Deeply

Restore Your Soul

JANET K. MARKS

ILLUMIFY
MEDIA.COM

INHALE

Copyright © 2023 by Janet K. Marks

All rights reserved. No part of this book may be reproduced in any form or by any means—whether electronic, digital, mechanical, or otherwise—without permission in writing from the publisher, except by a reviewer, who may quote brief passages in a review.

The views and opinions expressed in this book are those of the author and do not necessarily reflect the official policy or position of Illumify Media Global.

While there are lists of physical and emotional ailments in some chapters that can also be symptoms of depression, this book is not intended to provide mental health treatment and does not constitute a client/therapist relationship. Janet K. Marks is not a licensed psychologist.

Subscribe to newsletter at:

www.janetmarksauthor.com
Janet@janetmarksauthor.com

The names used in this book are fictional, unless otherwise noted.

Subjects: Spiritual Life. | Self-Reflection. | Personal Growth. | Overcoming. | Soul Care.

Back Cover Photo: Haylee Beth Photography

Published by
Illumify Media Global
www.IllumifyMedia.com
"*Let's bring your book to life!*"

Paperback ISBN: 978-1-959099-58-1

Typeset by Art Innovations (http://artinnovations.in/)
Cover design by Debbie Lewis

Printed in the United States of America

Dedication

For my mother, Marita Jean [Forney] Bornschlegel, who had the most beautiful soul.

"You are the finest, loveliest, tenderest, and most beautiful person I have ever known—and even that is an understatement." (F. Scott Fitzgerald)

Contents

A Note from the Author ix

PART ONE – INTANGIBLE SOUL 1
1. Jump Into the Deep End 5
2. Can My Soul Be Repaired? 15
3. Invitation to My Soul 21
4. If the Soul Could Speak 27

PART TWO – REFLECTIVE SOUL 35
5. The Practice of Stillness 41
6. The Practice of Quietness 49
7. The Art of Prayer 57

PART THREE – WOUNDED SOUL 63
8. How Do I Face My Scars? 71
9. I Am Not Alone 77
10. Rising From the Ashes 85
11. Surrendered Soul 93

PART FOUR – TRANSFORMED SOUL 101
12. Known by God 105
13. Uniquely You 111
14. Soul Bound 117
15. This Side of Heaven 125
16. Which Path? 131

PART FIVE – BEAUTIFUL SOUL 139

    17. An Honorable Soul 143
    18. A Grounded Soul 149
    19. The Steadfast Soul 155
    20. True Beauty 161

PSST, You Have a Beautiful Soul! 169

Acknowledgements 171

Notes 175

About the Author 177

A Note from the Author

WE ALL COME INTO THIS life gasping for air and then spend the rest of our years on this planet striving to make each breath matter. This book is a gentle guide to help you use *your breath* to slow, settle and contemplate the health of your soul.

If you are anything like me, deep inside, you yearn to have a vibrant soul and a meaningful connection with God. If life were perfect, there would be no wounds on your soul and no unease when looking deeper within. But life *isn't* perfect, and no one deals proficiently with all the issues that come along. We have some days that are so filled with joy they seem to glimmer like the hot summer sun. Others are intensely bitter, but for most of us our days are everything in between. When troubles arise, we are tempted to tuck them into the back of a closet, hoping beyond reason they will stay put. We falsely believe it will be easier to deal with those issues another time, or perhaps never.

Everyone knows that life is full of troubles. If you let them simmer and stew, if you do not address them head-on, you will only have more heartaches down the road. So instead of ignoring your spiritual injuries or bottling up fear, loneliness, anxiety, or bitterness, allow this book to help you breathe deeply and find health for your soul.

As you inhale long and full, strive for courage to dig deeper, talk truer and look further ahead to your dream of uncovering that beautiful soul.

Know that whether you feel

- *inadequate* in your connection with God,
- *uncertain* what your soul condition is,
- *wounded* in your soul and unsure how to get up again,
- *distressed* that your passion for God has flamed out, or
- *satisfied* and *at peace* with your connection to God,

wherever you stand spiritually, whatever may be trembling right now in your heart, remember this, God loves you and longs to restore this beautiful soul he placed within you.

My hope for you, dear reader, is that *INHALE* will be a torch to illuminate your journey and that you will be blessed in the reading.

Now, catch your breath.

Breathe in. Breathe out.

Release that tightness across your shoulders and pat yourself on the back for having bravely opened a book on deepening soul health.

PART ONE

Intangible Soul

"OH, GOD, I DON'T LOVE YOU. I don't even want to love you. But I want to want to love you."

Who of us cannot relate to the struggle expressed here by Theresa of Avila, a Carmelite nun who lived in the sixteenth century? She is known for her quiet approach to spirituality, yet she battled mightily to remain steady in her devotion.

We can't see God, we can't see our soul; it's no wonder we struggle to wrap our head around loving him or understanding the needs of our soul. Most of us *want* to love God, but sometimes it feels so out of reach that we stop trying. It's like riding a merry-go-round—horses go up, horses go down. Your love for God is up and feels pretty solid. Then without warning it plummets into uncertainty, and you question how to get it back.

The journey to love God is no smooth voyage. This ride we're on is nothing new.

Practically speaking, the idea of loving God with all your heart and soul is obscure and difficult to define. Because the soul is mostly indiscernible, it is hard to have anything but a shallow grasp of what soul health means. Sometimes we get frustrated and insecure about our spiritual progress because we *think* we should be farther along than we are. But to be fair, it's tough to manage what we cannot see or touch. It's hard enough to love those whom we can see. God is invisible, yet he implores us to love him with all our soul. No wonder we have questions.

The truth is, it's not easy to love a God who seems to stay out of your affairs except for the occasional moments of divine intervention, say for the near miss of a frightful car accident or a crystal clear answer to prayer.

On the days God feels hard to reach, I would rather ignore the pursuit and watch television or listen to music. I would prefer to do *anything* but dig around in the basement of my heart and unearth parts of my soul that need to be dealt with.

Writing this book revealed questions, concerns, and insecurities in my own walk with God and made me wonder how I could dare to be a voice for others to build their soul strength. I have been tempted to give up and declare the subject too elusive.

Like other God-followers, my journey with God has had numerous starts and stops, but I have also found that the more I share my doubts and struggles with fellow travelers, the more I understand that we are all in the same boat. These individuals have listened, shared their own issues, offered support, and have become safe shoulders on which to lean. What a comfort to have them walk beside me on this journey to better soul health.

Imprecise Pointing

Philip Yancey tells about receiving a letter from a friend as he wrote the remarkable book *Reaching for the Invisible God*. The friend, upon hearing Yancey's struggle to clearly depict God occasions of hidden-ness, wrote, "Every religious book is an imperfect finger pointing with indeterminable inaccuracy toward someone we cannot, by our pointing, make present."[1]

As I endeavor to point you toward achieving well-being in your soul, it seems an inconceivable role to play, and yet amazingly, God has allowed me to point! While my thoughts here are to help you inhale and breathe life into your soul, I use my imperfect finger to remind you of these truths:

- The one who created your mind allows you to doubt and even to say the words, "I don't love you."
- The God who made your soul isn't annoyed or offended by your hesitation but welcomes you with kindness despite your uncertainty.
- God understands how your soul has been injured and patiently and lovingly nudges you toward healing.
- He knows when you'd rather not think about weighty matters. He watches over you and waits for you to remember why you're here.
- He has given you rare and individual traits. Perhaps he's made you vivacious, ambitious, or tenacious. Maybe you are calm or loyal or possess great insight and patience. Whatever it is, he has poured distinctive gifts into your soul for a reason.

So whether you slog, stumble, or soar into soul health, the result can be a close, rewarding walk with God, made new and fresh every time the sun rises. He has placed these traits in you as a part of his divine plan to build a signature walk with you. Keep in mind, achieving this elusive "whole soul" is not a one-size-fits-all process, but in these pages you will find multiple tools to help your soul grow and thrive.

You will find questions at the end of each chapter to assist in further self-discovery. Use these prompts as a personal deep dive or jump over them and come back to them later. Also, the questions can be used in talking with a trusted friend or easily incorporated into a discussion group.

Even though "soul fitness" may be a new concept or feel unfamiliar, I urge you to lean into this fresh connection with God and know that nourishing your soul is never wasted time.

The goal of it all is to cultivate a healthy, beautiful soul.

1

Jump into the Deep End

"You are the only one who can make the decision to care for your soul."
—Ginger Harrington

AS A TEN-YEAR-OLD CHILD, I stood immobile at the foot of a tall ladder rising to the top of the highest high dive of the Jefferson County, Colorado, pool. A line of soggy, impatient divers behind me complained, "Hurry up, already!" Now that I was looking straight up the ladder, it was unthinkable that anyone in their right mind would climb up that tower and actually jump of their own volition. Not wanting to be labeled a chicken like Billy Miller (the poor guy had no escape from the hecklers once he climbed up and right back down earlier the same day), there was nothing to do but go forward.

In abject terror, stomach tense and heart racing, I hesitantly put my foot on the first rung, thinking wistfully of my towel laid out neatly under the sun umbrella. Up I went, my heartbeat elevating as the ground receded. At the top of the ladder, I thought I could see all the way to Kansas! Amongst the yells and jeers from the line behind me, I inched my way to the edge of the board, peered over, and saw my dad looking proud and waving in the water, clearly a mile below. In my head I wondered if anyone could spring off this platform and live. With the agitated kids behind me hollering, "Go! Go!

Go!" there was nothing to do but close my eyes, take a deep breath, and leap.

The next thing I knew, Dad was patting my back as I gasped for air, and sure enough, I lived to tell about the most death-defying belly flop ever. It stung like the dickens, but by golly I had done it. No chicken here!

Taking a Leap

What compels a person to take a leap into uncertainty? The motives for pushing past my fear included the dread of gaining an unfortunate label from my peers, a desire to make my dad proud, and bragging rights about my perilous plunge. Not a lot of deep thoughts crossed my mind. All I knew were the basics: climb the ladder, take a breath, and jump.

When we decide to cross a significant threshold, it is natural to inhale, square our shoulders, and go. A deep breath helps calm panicky nerves and level our emotions. Whether performing on a stage, walking down the aisle, or making any important decision, we breathe in, breathe out, and a surge of energy propels us forward.

Breathing doesn't seem complicated on the surface. Rarely do we even notice the simple in-and-out rhythm of our lungs, yet the intricacies are astonishing. Composed of specialized cells to extract oxygen from the atmosphere, our lungs draw in life-giving air. A chemical exchange floods oxygen to our blood cells, transforming them to accomplish essential functions throughout our body. We then expel carbon dioxide from the deep recesses of our lungs to make room for a fresh dose of oxygen. In an average human, this phenomenon occurs 12-18 times each minute, a whopping 23,000 times per day!

Let's dive deeper into an interesting spiritual parallel to taking a breath.

"Spiritual *inhaling*" can be compared to the times we stop to think about what sustains us, and to examine the true condition of our soul. We take a brief breath and determine how we might adjust some life choices.

Exhaling becomes the spiritual parallel to the "going and doing" of our lives. From sunrise to sunset, we expend energy for family, boss, neighbors, projects, home life, and other work. Sometimes it is easier to go full-throttle all day exhaling, *doing* things for others without stopping to *inhale* spiritual sustenance. But God did not design us to exhale only without facing dire consequences!

Deep Dive

A friend impressed me when for her sixtieth birthday, she trained for and competed in a seniors triathlon. The running and biking portions were less of a challenge for her, but the open water swim in the reservoir was quite difficult. The water was cold, dark, and murky. She had to push past her hesitance, get in the water and strive for her goal. If you have ever dived into a lake, you may understand her reluctance. The water is hazy, and you don't know what lurks below. The easy parallel to making a spiritual dive means you look willingly into the deeper shadowy recesses of your soul; you ask yourself questions and assess your motivations. Your first response may be to ignore such a dive but remember there is great benefit from a spiritual heart check. And like leaping into a lake, you take a big breath and go.

Also, it isn't enough to take a deep soul dive one day and then not do it again for a year. Developing a healthy soul requires faithful attention to the inner workings of our heart.

If I am unwilling to pause for self-reflection or tender touches of self-care, my well is apt to go dry, leaving me with little to share with those I care about.

The Trouble with Avoiding

A young professional woman asked me what I was writing. As I expounded on the value of soul health and frequent reflection on our hearts' condition, she knitted her eyebrows in dread. She shook her head and replied, "I felt bad about myself all through my youth and now I'm happy. Why would I ever want to look back at all that?" (As my dad always said, "Why open a can of worms?") She admitted she hadn't ever dealt with her painful past, and she knew it was still there no matter how much she avoided it. After some discussion, she agreed to give the issue some thought. That conversation helped me realize how much fear we sometimes experience as we face uncomfortable truths about our life stories.

If you relate to the hesitation of this woman, the concept of inspecting deeper areas of thought may intimidate you. If you are someone who tends to push away difficulties because they feel awkward, you are not alone. Many people are not eager to jump into the deep end of their souls. You may be tempted to climb back down the spiritual ladder, fearing the risk too great, or dreading what you might uncover upon self-reflection.

Soul-searching does not always come easy, but before you throw up your hands in dismay, I urge you to press on if you want to develop a healthy, beautiful soul. To accomplish this, you will need to learn how to be aware of areas lacking in your soul and to practice bravery as you face wounds deep within. You will become more aware of your spiritual needs through moments of self-reflection, taking a deep spiritual breath, if you will. Even though you may hesitate to take this spiritual breath and look closely into your soul, such spiritual inhaling is tremendous.

Who among us wouldn't prefer to splash around in the shallow end of the pool, ignoring the dark recesses of the deep end? At times, it seems the areas about which you feel embarrassed or ashamed are just too painful to approach. Or you might find yourself avoiding those who ask pertinent questions such as, "How are you doing, *really*?"

"Um."

So, you resist wading into the deep end; you find it simpler to cling to the side of the pool in a comfortable pattern of avoidance, hoping not to encounter any uncomfortable moments. Even though you long for a vibrant faith, you may fear what you will discover.

Avoidance is easy, and I get it.

The Benefit of Openness

When I am hurt, I typically grow quiet and stew. On one such occasion, after an arduous out-of-state move, my husband hurt my feelings. It was due to a small decision he made, but he didn't ask me about it and because I wanted to do it differently I became moody and mopey. It was obvious we needed to talk it over, but everything in me wanted to escape an uncomfortable conversation, to hide my pettiness, and *avoid* dealing with it. So, I pulled my heart back.

Avoidance feels somehow simpler and justified.

Everyone has caution tape stretched around portions of his or her heart, areas tough to approach. We do this for many reasons. Perhaps we have tried to tackle a particular area before with minimal success or we are dealing with an emotionally charged or tender topic. Instead of resolving the issue, we flit insecurely around its outer edges. You *know* you should address the matter, yet it feels easier to just evade it. But if you continue to dodge sensitive or challenging issues, one day you will wake up to a void, a place where your life lacks purpose, significant relationships have faltered, and there is little motivation to keep going.

Avoid leads to *a void*.

I knew I needed to speak up, but my typical excuses were squabbling in my head. *It's late. I'm tired and talking will not help. Plus, I am stupid to feel so hurt!* At some point in this brain-tangle, a voice said, *Do the right thing, Janet. Speak up. Stay kind. Be authentic.*

It started clumsily. I had a dry mouth and clammy hands. "Um, Babe, can we talk?" I asked. Generally, this is all it takes to start a conversation, but that first sentence is sometimes so hard to say, as if you've swallowed a mouthful of dry oats.

Tom's response was gentle, "Hon, I get it. We're going through a lot of new adjustments; and trying to get a lot accomplished. It isn't surprising we're both feeling emotions at every turn. But, we're in this together. We can figure it out."

We both apologized (me about overreacting, him about not considering my idea), we talked about the need for patience with each other and ourselves. We discussed the reality of our enemy who speaks lies at every turn, one who wants to defeat us and destroy any good in our lives. We determined, right in that moment, to do the right thing.

Our talk provided the reassurance I needed, that I would be heard and my opinion mattered. As we prayed together, I felt God nudge me to look below the surface of the situation and consider what truly mattered, the condition of my soul.

I took a deep breath and asked God for help. As I did, a verse I had read earlier that week came to mind: "Hear my voice when I call, O Lord, be merciful to me and answer. My heart says, 'Seek his face!' Your face, Lord, I will seek. Do not hide your face from me, do not turn your servant away in anger; you have been my helper" (Psalm 27:8-9).

I needed to consider what it meant for me to "seek his face," as this scripture suggested.

Not every conversation will go as smoothly, (apology, understanding, time in prayer and profound insight into my soul condition). It is wonderful when it does, but there are times you try to open up to someone, and they respond in anger or simply refuse to speak with you. Little issues grow big and can erupt. When accusations are thrown and conflict rages, we would all rather catch a cab right out of there! When the other party is not being reasonable, your patience will be tested. Though you will be tempted to escalate or rage back, this will never improve the situation. This is the time to excuse yourself, distance yourself from the circumstances, get input from a trusted objective party, and pray to love like God does.

Everyone has experienced conflict, and (almost) no one likes it. But by slowing down and taking deep breaths, you can approach the scuffle with calmness, strive to use better conflict resolution skills, and promote smoother communication. Slowing down and breathing deeply will help you think clearer and address the issue. And as always, remember, it is your heart's desire to grow and strengthen your soul.

Sadly, avoidance patterns can become a habit. They may be helpful in reducing pain for the time-being, but if issues remain unchecked, you will sense a void, *something* that is missing, because you are evading what really matters. Also, if you blame others for your problems and refuse to take responsibility, the opportunity to grow and mature will be greatly diminished. If you won't make time for self-reflection, you sacrifice self-awareness, which allows shallowness to become your standard. The end result of avoiding scary feelings may lead to superficiality in your relationships and more awkwardness and fear.

In her book *The Dance of Fear* Dr. Harriet Lerner writes, "It is not fear that stops you from doing the brave and true thing in your daily life. Rather the problem is *avoidance*. You want to feel comfortable, so you avoid doing or saying the thing that evokes fear."

How true this is.

We fear gazing into the reflection pool of our soul, so we busy ourselves and steer clear of any moments to ponder our truth. Giving in to your discomfort may yield a few drops of relief but often ends in a deluge of emptiness. Dr. Lerner continues, "Avoidance will make you feel less vulnerable in the short run, but it will *never* make you less afraid."

In a nutshell, avoiding an issue due to fear will not resolve the issue, and it will never make you less afraid to resolve it.

Take a slow, deep breath now. As you consider your soul, peek around those corners you sometimes keep hidden and pray:

> *Dear God of my soul, help me find the courage to wade a little further into the deep end. I know there are areas of my heart I tend to ignore, thoughts I push away and conversations I avoid, but I want my soul to be healthy and I know this is the way forward. Help me trust that you will remain by my side as I take these steps. Amen.*

Breathing Deeper

1. What does it mean for you to seek God's face?
2. What words would you use to describe your current spiritual condition?
3. In what ways do you look past or avoid areas about which you are fearful?

2

Can My Soul Be Repaired?

"You are a beautiful masterpiece; your life is a work of art."
—June Saruwatari

OVER FIVE HUNDRED YEARS AGO Leonardo Da Vinci began work on one of history's most influential paintings, *The Last Supper*. This famous work allegedly depicts the moments just following Jesus' stunning revelation that someone in their midst would betray him that night. The painting displays the shock and anger of the apostles sitting with him at the table.

In the last half of the twentieth century a team of specialists undertook the painstaking process of restoring this magnificent work of art. The piece had undergone several botched restorations over the years and was sadly exposed to the elements during World War II. No one believed a true renewal could be accomplished.

The restorers worked tirelessly in small sections of the colossal fifteen-by-twenty-nine-foot painting to remove layers of previous retouching attempts, blankets of dirt and grime, and coats of varnish. Using microscopic photography and infrared and sonar technology, the renovation took two decades and millions of dollars to complete.

Why all the effort? Why the expense and dedication? Why try to bring back something so badly damaged? Simply stated, the painting is a masterpiece and is considered one of the greatest paintings in the world.

Your soul is a masterpiece. As hard as it may be to comprehend, *you* are his work of art! "For we are God's masterpiece. He has created us anew in Christ Jesus, so we can do the good things he planned for us long ago" (Ephesians 2:10, NLT). "We" means "You." It bears repeating: *You* are God's masterpiece! You are created by God and regardless of how damaged your soul may be, you are worth his efforts to restore you.

Ode to My Soul

God created your soul and will restore you masterfully; you were created for a purpose. Look at the Greek word for masterpiece: *Poiema*. This word means "poem or poetry" in English and is the word used in this scripture. The beauty in you is God's poetry. You are God's Poem!

When someone reminds me to grasp my value in God's eyes, it is common to hear a "Yes, but" rolling off my tongue. I want to explain all the reasons why I am not special and clarify that due to my poor choices he couldn't possibly love me. But when I stop my excuses and allow the truth to flow over me, hope wells up like a bright yellow balloon, a beautiful reminder that God really does love me and is eager to show me my worth.

The soul was his idea.

He will not allow your soul to be broken beyond repair. His plan has always been for you to be redeemed and to restore you back to an authentic connection with him.

You are God's work of art, his masterpiece, his poem.

Consider the significance of this scripture: "One day the Eternal God scooped dirt out of the ground, sculpted it into the shape we call human, breathed the breath that gives life . . . and the human became a living soul." (Genesis 2:7, VOICE). God is the creator of the soul. He, who breathed life into us can also satisfy and heal our souls. The soul placed within you is God's divine light, as shown here: "The spirit of a person is the lamp of the Lord, searching all the innermost parts of his being" (Proverbs 20:27, NASB). God placed a soul within you to see *you*. His invisible spirit can see your invisible spirit like a bright star in the night sky. When the light reveals a hard truth in your heart, his intention is to help, to mend what is broken. What a gift that he is willing to repair your soul with love and compassion and not let it stay broken!

You matter to God.

One of the most quoted verses in the Bible is a reminder of his desire to restore you. "The Lord is my Shepherd, I shall not want. He makes me lie down in green pastures; He leads me beside quiet waters. He restores my soul." (Psalm 23:1-3 NASB). That means, in whatever condition you find yourself, God, the Shepherd, is right by your side. Not only did he create your soul, but he promises to renew it. He wants this relationship.

Think of the many ways he has "knocked on your door" or called out to you through people or circumstances. He uses various scenarios to grab your attention, whether from breathtaking beauty in nature to breath-snatching adversity, he keeps tapping so you'll notice he's there.

To fathom God's intricate plan for soul restoration, we need to begin to grasp what soul health means. The concept of the soul can be elusive. It is not easy to point your finger and say about the soul, *This is it* or *There it goes*. Our soul has an imperceptible essence; you know it's there, but it is hard to grasp, like recalling a dream upon awakening.

Soul care may be confused with *self-care*, a popular catchword on magazine covers seen at the checkout lane, but these terms are not the same. We are not talking about binging on "prime time me time" or sleeping in every day (although, if you need extra sleep or time to relax, you should take it). It isn't the whiney "What about me?" self-care you read about in self-absorbed blog posts. Merriam-Webster defines *soul* as "the spiritual principle embodied in human beings, all rational and spiritual beings, or the universe."

The struggle for a healthy soul may feel elusive, but any effort you make to ensure a vibrant soul is well worth it. It is feasible to keep your soul in top condition if you heed the areas needing improvement. Listen for how God nudges you forward, and allow him to restore the places deep within.

Oh! To experience that undeniable connection with God!

Whole Soul

Restore means "To reestablish or bring back a previous condition, to make good."

Have you ever watched the contractors on television shows like *This Old House* and marveled at how they can transform a broken-down old house? It is inspiring to watch the "reveal" to see the transformation of the old home into something astonishing and valuable. The place is typically taken back to its bare bones, even to the foundation, and then rebuilt better than before. What about that old piece of furniture on the show *Fixer Upper*? We stare in awe as a scraped and dented piece of furniture is stripped to bare wood, given a shiny new finish, and made beautiful and valuable.

The theme of restoration is woven throughout Scripture, and every time God makes *better* that which he touches. He is the Master Craftsman. So, considering what you know about restoration, what might it look like when God refurbishes your soul?

More than likely, God's restoration will involve greater detail than slapping on a fresh coat of paint. He may strip away your walls of self-protection to expose the harmful inclinations of your soul. He knows how to gently remove detrimental dirt and grime and assure you will be structurally sound. The process can be painful, but God restores you to peaceful places, (still waters and green pastures). He will take all the time he needs to retouch and restore you to the best possible *you*.

God is not only the Creator of your soul but the Lover of your soul as well. His masterpiece (you) will stand the test of time!

Someone asked me if God's part and mine are equal in soul restoration. It's a valid question. God is bigger and stronger than me, so does that mean more is expected from him? It could be answered by another question: Which is more important, the left or right wing of an airplane? As my sister put it, "God in his innate power gives everything he can, and I in my innate weakness give everything I can." Both sides play a part. But on your side, only you can control your efforts to remain in good spiritual shape.

Stop and bask in God's acceptance of your bent and broken soul. In this place of slowing, allow your walls to come down and lay your burdens at his feet. Pray this now:

> *My God, how can it be that I am your masterpiece? Hearing that my soul is like a poem to you touches me deeply. Help me listen closely for your voice as you build and restore my soul. Put me in a frame of mind where your love will connect with my soul. Amen.*

Breathing Deeper

1. The struggle for soul health seems hard and sometimes elusive. Why is it worth the effort?
2. God created your soul. What area of your life needs his kind restoration?
3. You are God's poem. In what ways does this concept motivate you to keep you soul in good condition?

3

Invitation to My Soul

"No one will ever fully understand…the deepest recesses of your mind, heart and soul. God himself is the answer to the fulfillment, only he himself can fill the longing heart."
—Virginia Brandt Berg

A FEW YEARS AGO, SEVERAL of us stood in a noisy crowd cheering the weary runners nearing the final stretch of the Austin Marathon. We were waiting at the finish line and finally saw our daughter's neon purple outfit flash around the last corner of the route, her glassy eyes fixed on her target. Jessica had been diligently putting one foot in front of the other for 26.2 miles despite intense hip pain in the final four. We screamed our lungs out urging her to finish strong. Later, she told me she heard the melee but dared not take her eyes off the goal.

When a physical body has used up so much energy that it nears depletion, it is a struggle to take even one more step; the body aches to be replenished. After the race, Jessica needed to take time to rest, hydrate, and nourish her body to recuperate and regain her strength.

Your soul is no different. For replenishment, your soul requires sustenance and essential support such as spiritual rest, living water, and the bread of life. It is never fun to admit that your soul is drained, but you won't maintain a healthy soul if you ignore its depletion.

Your soul was never designed to run on empty!

Spiritual DNA

When you are thirsty, you yearn for water. When you are hungry, your belly feels hollow, and you sense a strong urge to fill it. Built into your DNA is a strong survival instinct to replenish and nourish.

Your spiritual DNA functions the same way. Though there is no rumbling, no clock announcing it is lunchtime, if you are attentive, you can also sense when your soul is hungry.

If you don't know exactly what your soul is hungering for, simply

slow down,
take time to reflect and consider your soul condition,
and *ask* God to reveal which areas of your soul need nourishment or attention today.

In the wilderness, God provided manna for the hungry and irritable Israelites. (Who hasn't experienced being cranky when hungry? When I get this way, my husband encourages me to have a little snack.) God instructed them to gather only enough manna for what they needed for that day and nothing extra. It was a lesson in trust and dependence on God. His promise to them and to you is this, "He satisfies the thirsty and fills the hungry with good things" (Psalm 107:9).

What a gift from the Creator of your soul. He offers to refresh you, to slake your thirst and fill your emptiness.

God placed a yearning in us. It's his design that causes our soul to crave things. Like a narrow chasm scooped out of the earth, we long for God to show up, flow in, and spill over. God placed this need inside you to be filled.

The Offer

An old preacher was once asked to talk about special moments he'd had in prayer. He scratched at his scruffy beard and said, "Best prayer I ever prayed was one day hanging upside-down off a ladder!" Now, that's an honest answer! We pray our best prayers when our soul is overwhelmed.

Contrary to human thinking, this doesn't surprise God, nor offend him. When we are in frantic circumstances, it is right to cry out for help. When we face tough situations, our first instinct is to cry out to God for relief. There are times when no human can help. When you have nowhere else to turn, don't assume he doesn't care. Turn to God. He is *always* there for you. He understands you and invites you into his presence and, no matter what craziness is happening, he ministers to you and wants to remind you he is near.

Everyone faces spiritual exhaustion and impossible difficulty at times. This is the exact moment Jesus offers this morsel: "Come to me, all you who are weary and burdened, and I will give you rest" (Matthew 11:28).

Do you hear the gentleness? This is the offer: peace of mind and reassurance to your weary soul. The rest he speaks of is an invitation to slow your pace, readjust your focus, and lean on him—lean on him for strength, for comfort, and for perseverance. Despite the numerous pressures you face, here in this moment, you can come to him and bask in his perfect plan to resupply what is lacking.

The Message version of the Bible states the same verse with a refreshing twist: "Get away with me and you'll recover your life. I'll show you how to take a real rest . . . Learn the unforced rhythms of grace."

What an offer! What a beautiful depiction of God's promise of acceptance. He never forces you to follow him but patiently waits for you to come to him.

If you're like me, on the days my soul is in poor shape, weary, or fraught with indifference, the thought of learning "the unforced rhythms of grace" sounds completely unattainable and far away. But the idea put forth in this scripture is this: When my soul is spent, he simply bids me to draw near.

"Come to me."

Wow! He wants me near!

Very little is required for you to *come* to the Lord; just your willingness to slow down, give him your burdens, and trust him with your soul.

The Summons

This beautiful depiction from Psalms declares, "As the deer pants for streams of water, so my soul pants for you, O God. My soul thirsts for God, the living God" (Psalm 42:1-2). This may sound like the words to a melodic song, but as we read further the writer asks, "Why, my soul, are you downcast? Why so disturbed within me?" (Psalm 42:5). The writer is tormented by some unknown scenario.

But then, the writer continues, "Deep calls to deep in the roar of your waterfalls; all your waves and breakers have swept over me" (Psalm 42:7). "Deep calls to deep." In moments of anxiety or disillusionment, the deepest part of you calls out to the deepest part of God. What a vision! When your thirst needs to be quenched and your soul longs to be filled, it is natural for your deep to call to God's deep.

Some commentators assert that the waterfall, waves, and breakers may be a metaphor for what is causing the writer's dismay. Possibly, but what if we consider another viewpoint?

Could there be any more refreshing thought for someone thirsty and panting in a desert than to come to a waterfall or to have breakers at the shore wash over them? What a blessing to one who is thirsty!

Inhale and fill your lungs, draw strength from his desire to connect. He will quench your thirst and satisfy your deepest longings. Know he hears you when you pray:

> *God, quiet my heart and let me be still enough to hear your "deep" calling to mine. When my soul feels parched, please replenish and refresh me within. Help me lean on you today and rest in your amazing "unforced rhythms of grace." Help me to breathe in your peace and trust your perfect plan. Amen.*

Breathing Deeper

1. How do you respond to the gentle offer from Jesus, "Come to me and I will give you rest?" What kind of rest is he offering you?
2. Your soul was never designed to run on empty. In what ways do you need to be filled?
3. God placed a yearning in you. What do you hunger for in your spiritual life?

4

If the Soul Could Speak

"Through pride we are ever deceiving ourselves. But deep down below the surface of the average conscience a still, small voice says to us, something is out of tune."
—C. G. Jung

IF YOUR SOUL COULD SPEAK out loud, what might it say? Would you hear, "Hey, a little help over here. I'm weary, running on empty!" Like the gas gauge of your car indicating the fuel is low means it's time to fill 'er up!

Or, when the check engine light starts blinking on the dashboard, we clearly understand there is a concern. No one believes the car will get better on its own if we ignore the warning—though based on personal experience, often we hope this to be true. We think, "Maybe that blinking light will just go away." When it has been signaling a long time with no apparent consequences, we might not even notice it anymore until something major happens.

Last year my trusty Honda started acting strangely. As I accelerated, there was a hesitation, a tiny lurch. The accelerator didn't respond as it normally did. Maybe, I reasoned, it was my shoe, the road, or anything else besides an issue with the car. So, I ignored it.

My son borrowed it the next weekend and mentioned, "It's driving kind of funny." I chose to believe it was probably just him, but after a few weeks, the lurching became more pronounced.

It was obvious now, the car needed work. After I dropped it off I was led to a holding area to wait for the diagnosis. After sipping on tepid coffee and being subjected to nearly an hour of some inane game show, the mechanic appeared and told me my car had the "jutters!" That sounded pretty serious! Anticipating the worst, I braced myself. Then he said, "Good news! It can be fixed!" He replaced some fluids, and now it runs like new.

It's not so different when it comes to maintaining your soul. How long can you neglect that blinking red light? Or the lurching? When you get the spiritual jutters and know something is off, you might rather ignore it or pretend there is no problem. Since you have no blinking red light on your head (unless you are Rudolph the reindeer), how can you discover the condition of your soul?

Deeper spiritual problems often send signals to you, sometimes physically, sometimes emotionally. Note the two following lists of ways your soul may be speaking to you.

Physically you may notice:

- You feel more weakness than wellness or an overarching malaise that you can't put your finger on.
- You may experience stomach discomfort, headaches, shortness of breath or other unexplained maladies.
- You are easily overwhelmed with daily tasks, unable to complete projects or find solutions.
- You sleep more than expected, your sleep patterns become erratic, or you "check out" for hours at a time.
- You adopt a hectic schedule to avoid thinking about deeper problems.

Emotionally you may recognize:

- You engage in constant negative self-talk.
- You feel discouraged, purposeless, or struggle to find the good in life.
- You avoid hard conversations.
- You try to press on without resolving conflict.
- You ignore issues and hope they will go away.
- You dodge those who ask meaningful questions, fearing what may be exposed.

If you recognize any of these or similar clues, don't freak out. These are just a few check-your-soul signals that communicate a need. Don't judge yourself harshly, and certainly don't give up. Instead, acknowledge there may be a deeper problem, take a good look, and then ask God to help you find the necessary steps to regain your spiritual footing. And take heart! He can fix it! Everyone goes through periods where we need refreshing. You are not alone.

When God stirs something in your soul, when flares are being sent out, how well do you sit up and listen? Do you ignore the signals or try to pretend they are not there? They might be a hint to open your eyes to the condition of your soul. It is possible that you already know some of what is going on inside, but you have buried or blocked it out. If you are open to it, these little signals can help you get unblocked and free again.

It is *never* convenient when a warning signal lights up the dashboard. Accepting that your soul may be in turmoil or a negative state can be challenging. But please remember this: it never helps to ignore those pesky promptings.

Voice of the Soul

One day I sat at my computer attempting to write but felt blocked by frustration fizzing under the surface. I felt someone had blown off a scheduled telephone appointment and I was, well, annoyed. Staring at the blinking cursor only aggravated me more. I had a deadline looming, and there was no time for a wasted morning.

So I scolded myself, "Get a grip. Get over it!"

I didn't.

Self-pity thickened around my heart as I worried I had been forgotten. No amount of self-flagellation or self-talk would make it go away. Feeling forgotten made me feel unimportant, which led to more stewing and even less writing. Finally, it became clear that I would accomplish no coherent work until something changed. I shut down the computer and went in to clean the kitchen. (There may have been some banging of pots and pans and cupboard doors.)

But then I asked myself, "What am I missing?" I had been keenly ignoring the beacons of blinking lights my soul was sending up.

It's funny how we try any workaround to avoid facing our inner truth. We ignore issues, scold ourselves, or get angry at someone. I had the spiritual jutters but kept lurching down the road instead of addressing the problem.

There was a super-sized snarl in my head, but I couldn't grasp the thread. A thought occurred to me that I should look deeper into the condition of my soul not just my outward circumstance of frustration.

Finally, I sat down (slowed) and asked God to show me what was going on (took time to consider my soul's condition). I asked him to soothe my agitated emotions so I could hear what was causing the turbulence in my soul (listened).

Deep down, there was more bothering me than the imagined snub of a missed phone call. Since we have moved frequently, I lack deep roots anywhere. Oh, how I would like to not have to find a new doctor again, new stores, new neighbors, and just be in a place where everyone knows my name. (There is a catchy song going through my head right now.) Most of it is just jutters in my head. But the issues must be dealt with, or there will be real-life consequences. My reaction to the missed phone appointment was just a flare sent up by my soul to say, "Um, a little attention over here!"

If you are like me, such emotions grow long, boney fingers that reach in and choke out joy. Once the knots were revealed, I could allow God to untangle them one by one. I called a friend, listened to some music, prayed, and tried to surrender. A calmness came over me, not because I didn't feel neglected anymore but because I listened to what my soul was signaling, and God filled my heart with reassurance of his love and his presence.

I have complained to God on numerous occasions about not feeling like I fit in anywhere. Moving to a new place invariably dredges up bouts of loneliness. He answers gently with reminders that where I currently reside is not my final destination. In heaven, *everyone* knows my name. (And yours!)

What are the thoughts that call you out of your gloom? What are the beliefs you hold onto that keep you from going over the edge? Find your words of faith and hold them close to your heart. Say words, such as:

> I believe God is there even when I struggle to see him.
> I know God loves me even when I doubt or when I pout.
> God is working to lead my life the way he knows it should go.

God made my soul, and he desires to renew me.
God wants me close.

What other words of faith are meaningful to you? Contemplate this concept of the psalmist's response to God: "Because he bends down to listen, I will pray as long as I have breath!" (Psalm 116:2, NLT). Like a parent leaning down to the child's level, can you visualize God bending down to listen to all that is burning in your soul? Feel him soothe and lift you up as a loving parent.

Dallas Willard, an American philosopher who wrote extensively about the concept of soul care, explains in his book *Renovations of the Heart*, "Once we clearly acknowledge the soul, we can learn to hear its cries."[2] Learning to recognize the voice of your soul, and listening in whatever form it uses to signal to you, involves close and careful attention. Like being awakened by the sound of an unexpected bump outside your window, there is a moment when you instinctively incline your head and lean in, waiting to hear it again. You must discern if it is friend or foe. When you realize it is just an empty pizza box being tossed along by the wind, you exhale with a sigh of relief and slip back to sleep.

A similar focus is needed to discern the health of your soul. Listen closely. Bend in to hear. Refrain from tuning out what may feel uncharted or unexpected. As you pay close attention, your ears become more attuned to the true condition of your soul. It takes more than your physical ears to hear when your soul is speaking. Rumi, a Persian poet from the thirteenth century said, "Close your ears and listen!" Quiet the outside noises, focus within, and give ear to thoughts deeper than sound. There is immense value in contemplating and considering what God is signaling to you through your soul.

And there is a great difference between the words *hearing* and *listening*. Just as it takes more than physical ears to hear what is going on in your soul, it takes more than physical eyes to see. Note the difference between the two words *sight* and *insight*. They signify vastly different concepts. Which is preferable for "seeing" your soul's needs?

Fine-Tuning Your Soul

Before any opera, ballet, symphony, or musical production, the audience is subjected to sounds of chaos as the members of the orchestra fine tune their instruments. The violins whine, trumpets squawk, and the oboe blares its scales up and down. None of the members is attempting to be in tune with the others. No one questions this or finds it off putting. But if the instruments are out of tune once the show is underway, they have a big problem.

Tuning an instrument is about the small details rather than the broad strokes. Once the orchestra begins to play, each performer must carefully listen to ensure harmony. Tuning in on the voice of the soul requires nothing less. You practice, you adjust, and you listen closely to the notes being played. Your ability to truly "hear" will improve with practice.

Developing a beautiful soul takes patience, practice, and listening to small details. You must tune your soul carefully to God's heart. You learn, you grow, and you find ways to hit the notes more consistently.

Quiet your thoughts, lean in close, and listen. As you discover what troubles your soul today, take steps to adjust. Breathe in the promises of God and let them smooth the rough places as you pray:

O God, incline my heart to bravely face the "check engine" light of my soul and to pay closer attention to what it is saying. Sometimes I am afraid to look inside, afraid to see the areas where I am weak. Please breathe new life into my soul, open my ears to hear and my eyes to see. Teach me to respond with my life. Amen.

Breathing Deeper

1. What *physical* indications do you notice in yourself when your soul needs some attention? What are the *emotional* indicators?
2. When you are agitated or discontented, what will remind you to stop and ask God to show you what is going on in your soul?
3. How do you bend in close to hear the voice of your soul? In which ways do you tune out what feels unfamiliar? How can you tune your ears to be more in harmony to the true condition of your soul?

PART TWO

Reflective Soul

A TALENTED WOMAN I SPOKE with struggled *for years* to look at herself in the mirror. She didn't like what she saw, so she averted her eyes. This presented some problems for her since there are mirrors in every home, store, and restroom. She once spoke with a therapist about this fierce dislike of looking at herself and admitted to him, with no small amount of embarrassment, that she always washed her hands standing sideways so she wouldn't have to look at herself in the mirror.

Obviously, she faced quite a dilemma for wherever she went so went her reflection. Sadly for her, every glance was a reminder of her failings—thousands of reminders!

It wasn't that she had some visible flaw. She was a typical-looking young mom. She was sociable and successful. But as we know all too well, fears, insecurities, and aversions don't discriminate.

Learning to be reflective when it comes to soul health intimidates most of us. Whatever it is we hope to avoid when we look deep within, like a child who imagines monsters in the closet, we must acknowledge the fact that we sometimes presume our troubles to be more terrible than they are.

The woman made headway in her recovery through a daily practice of looking directly in a mirror, making faces at herself, darting in and out of view, and watching herself dance around. Her therapist had suggested this as a visual reminder that the woman had much to offer: wisdom, compassion, humor, and a deeply caring heart. If she could realize her inner qualities and see them reflected in the mirror, she may become less fearful.

Contemplation

As you dive into the reflecting pool of the heart, ask yourself a few questions:

- Does it make me nervous to think about probing the deeper recesses of my soul?
- Do I hope my issues remain undisturbed if I look away and ignore them?
- Do I fear that people in my life will find out I am not perfect?

News flash! They already know!

Why tromp through your days hiding your heart, thinking no one will see your flaws? Every single person has pieces of their lives they would rather keep out of sight, but remember, those issues are not a measure of your *value* to God.

Take a moment to acknowledge that every person is far from perfect. Don't let your anxiety about looking deeper into your soul keep you from personal growth or let it stunt your spiritual formation. Try not to look at your soul with broken human vision but rather see it as God does: precious, unique, and unrivaled.

Perhaps, like me, you have prayed superficially to grow spiritually, not really being aware of your imperfections. One day our preacher read a scripture I had heard many times about forgiveness. And like a bird flying happily through the trees that suddenly whomps into a window, the scripture he quoted stopped me in my tracks. I sat there in my Sunday best utterly gob smacked, knowing there was a woman whom I had refused to forgive.

For ~~weeks~~ months I had been unwilling to look closely at this hamstrung relationship. I had allowed a bitter kernel to be stashed neatly into a downstairs closet of my heart. I had ignored the issue but God had not. He showed me loud and clear through one man's voice, with a short verse mentioned in a little church on a cold December morning.

Try as I may, I could not shove it back into its cubby. It was clear I needed some perspective, so later that day I called my dear sister and told her I needed help.

"Okaaaay," she said, drawing out the word, unsure what I was about to say. The situation spilled out in one long breath as I uttered what I didn't want to admit, that bitterness was winning the battle in my heart! She was quiet for a moment and then gently asked, "Um, aren't you writing a book about breath for the wounded soul and praying for God to expose the depths of your own?"

Gulp. "Yes." Oh, it bites and stings to admit it when we see this kind of flaw in ourselves.

A helpful conversation followed, filled with her kind advice. She encouraged me to ask God to help me let go of my bitterness and forgive. Then she asked me what I could learn from the situation (since God had placed this woman in my life) and reminded me that such situations help me truly love like Jesus.

Sigh.

Willing myself to think about my attitude toward the woman was hard because the uncomfortable truth about my soul's condition embarrassed, humiliated, and frustrated me.

God used my sister to help point me in the right direction as I faced what was buried deep in my heart.

We don't often pray to be shown the truth about our deepest selves because it is so incredibly hard to face it. Whenever resentment or bitterness (or any dreadfulness) is uncovered, we want to be rid of it, but we aren't naturally motivated to do so. Do you sometimes feel too weak, resistant, or overwhelmed to even think about it?

You may be unsure how to go about changing the not-so-pretty attitudes buried inside. Maybe you believe those aspects of your personality are unrepairable, or you are just despondent from trying and failing. Could it be you keep dealing with the same struggles over and over and simply feel out of your league in knowing how to make a true change?

You tell yourself that if you stay busy enough you can ignore the difficulties and hope they won't show up again.

Except they do. They always show up.

Introspection

Becoming self-aware is the first step toward creating positive change. This comes about through introspection, which is the act or process of examining your thoughts and your motives.

Taking time to contemplate all that lies in your heart will give you the insight as to why you think or behave as you do. More important, the practice helps you develop a more authentic and unguarded soul. Here are just a few positive results you will gain through *honest* soul-searching:

1. Deepened self-awareness.

Explore your experiences, interactions, and challenges. As you do, reflect on your faith, your reactions, your relationships, and any long-buried issues nestled deep in the folds of your mind. Once you determine what is holding you back you can address it more effectively.

2. Better equipped to recognize your inconsistencies.

Like most people, you have a fairly strong sense of what kind of person you want to be, so when you look closely at your soul's condition, there is a good chance you will see shortcomings, bad habits, or negative impulses. There will be areas about which you do not feel proud, areas that do not reflect who you want to be.

When you discover an undesirable tendency, don't hide it away in a dark cave! It won't go away. Instead, it will become worse and cause additional problems. This is the time to bravely shine the light brighter and begin to make profound shifts in your behavior.

3. More humility about your spiritual condition.

Humility involves a willingness to honestly evaluate your abilities, beliefs, and privileges. As you genuinely search your soul, learn to accept your weaknesses but also acknowledge your strengths. Be humble about what you discover and allow trusted individuals to know the inner workings of your heart.

4. Enhanced connection with others.

As you grow in seeing yourself more clearly, oddly, it helps you become *less* self-involved. It places you in a frame of mind to be attuned to the needs of others and thereby more deeply connected.

Relax into the idea of introspection. Think about the benefits that will come as you are in touch with the truth of your own heart. Breathe into these next chapters. Do not fear what you might find but trust God to reveal exactly what you need right now and breathe life into your soul.

5

The Practice of Stillness

"All of humanity's problems stem from man's inability to sit quietly in a room alone."
—Blaise Pascal

ABSOLUTE GOOD CAN BE FOUND if we learn to stop and take a moment to consider what matters most. I don't know if *all* the problems of mankind stem from our inability to sit quietly as Pascal asserts, but it is true that in all our running and panting from one thing to the next, we lose our ability to pay attention to what matters most.

Learning to be self-reflective means you develop a habit of stillness. It can be as simple as sitting quietly and allowing your thoughts to settle, to "check-in," and to evaluate the significance of your soul condition.

If this idea is new for you, start small. Take five to ten minutes to sit with your thoughts, away from screens and distractions. A physical reminder may help signal that it is time to settle and be reflective. For example, you might light a candle, open the window shade to let in the daylight, feel for your heartbeat, hold a warm cup of tea, or do a few slow stretches. I know someone who does a thought dump. To clear his mind, he writes a quick list of all his whirling thoughts and sets it aside to deal with later. Then he can dive deeper into his self-reflective moments.

Keep in mind, there are days when grabbing even a minute of quiet feels completely outside of the realm of possibility. I spoke with a mother of two small children who attempted to get up earlier to have time for reflection, but the smell of a dirty diaper distracted her. After addressing that, the kids were up and raring to go and her moment was lost. It happens.

Sometimes increased work duties bring a build-up of emails pinging on the phone. It can be a struggle to set them aside to be still with deeper thoughts. Those traveling for business, running for flights, and sleeping in hotel rooms often have no rhythm on which to depend. If this is you, you will need to get imaginative. Talk with others who seek soul health, learn from them and share what works for you.

We all have days when obstacles press in from every side; no one is immune. But you will become better equipped with practice and creativity. Try to foresee the time and place:

Time: As you evaluate your personal situation, you can usually settle on a time that is less likely to be interrupted.

Place: Place is equally important. Attempt to find a quiet location where you will be less likely to be disrupted. If you struggle to find a favorite place, use your mind to picture where you'd love to be. Can you imagine sitting at the beach on a summer morning and smelling the fresh salt air blowing past? Or sitting in a beautiful park and staring up at the cobalt sky?

Whenever you make the time and whatever place of peace you find, allow these moments to help open your heart.

A woman I know who is the president of a multi-million-dollar company rises very early each morning, pours herself a cup of coffee, then sits silently for several minutes awaiting God's prompts for the day. She calls it her 4:30 Chair. It is a routine she does not abandon even when her days are packed full and teeming with tasks. The diligence she exhibits to maintain her own well-being is a great example for any of us who think we are too busy or distracted to be still.

There are many ways to incorporate the practice of slowing. The key is actually *to do it*.

Don't give up when you fail.

Don't quit because it's hard.

Soul health doesn't come easy to any of us. At times we are feeble and unsure how to stop. Other times we are simply stubborn and unwilling to slow down and learn the rhythm of stillness. It requires strong determination to stay open to God's gentle nudges. (Also, has anyone besides me noticed that if you ignore a gentle nudge, it becomes a sharp elbow in your side?) To better respond to these little pushes and prods, just pull away from the chaos, still your mind, and pray for insight. Keep in mind, if you don't learn from what life brings your way, you may find yourself standing in the exact same spot trying to process the same lesson over and over again.

Becoming aware of your failings is the perfect time to invite God in and ask him to restore and mend your broken places. It is absolutely the best time to ask for help.

It takes a certain resolve to sit in stillness and take deep spiritual breaths, but never forget God's intent is to strengthen your spirit. Not all people are willing to inhale fresh breaths and new thoughts, but since you are holding this book in your hands, you are not those people! You have the heart to develop a beautiful soul.

Being still doesn't mean not moving, it means finding opportunities and rhythms to slow down, and lovingly give yourself time to learn.

Stillness may be your best move today.

Soul in Repose

Learning how to slow down and still your thoughts is well worth your time and will prepare you for whatever may come your way. At first glance the idea of a soul in repose seems to mean "restful" and "peaceful." But in my research, I found two opposing thoughts on the definition of the word *repose*.

On one hand, we find a soothing description of repose that involves stillness, ease, and calmness. On the other hand, from a geological standpoint, *repose* is a period between eruptions of a volcano, as in "a volcano in repose." Who wants to hunker down in that place, never knowing when the next belch of destruction will spew out? It sounds nerve-racking and not calm at all.

Which of these two ideas best defines your repose? Do you dwell in a place of calm or is your life better described as living from volcano to volcano, hoping to catch your breath between eruptions? If it is the latter, it doesn't sound much like the placid place of repose you might be wishing for.

Keep in mind, no life is void of occasional volcanic bursts. But the hope is to develop healthier patterns of response to these challenges, so you can enjoy days, weeks, and even years without having volcanoes serve as bookends.

I once saw a mug with a simple inscription that made me tilt my head and say, "Wow!"

She found silence. For today it was a breath, one lovely deep breath.
Yesterday it was a moment, drinking tea alone when she noticed the steam curling up.
She decided to watch for pockets like this every day, to plan for them even.
To enter them like she might the doorway of a friend.
(Kay Noelle)

Do you watch for pockets of peacefulness? In the stillness, in a breath or even in a wisp of steam rising from your tea? If you open your eyes and look, you may be surprised about the moments of tranquility you find in the most ordinary places.

God knows the volcanoes that are threatening. He knows what is rumbling in your heart. Take moments to be still, to calm yourself and watch for his presence; let him rejuvenate your spiritual life through simple everyday pockets.

The Humble Rest Note

Once, a friend remarked how challenging it is for her to sit in any one place for any amount of time. She goes full throttle for days on end, sometimes to the point of illness and then is forced to rest. This is a typical cycle for many.

Is it in your DNA to run full tilt, willy-nilly until you fall over from exhaustion? Are you afraid you will miss some spectacular moment? Are you afraid to stop?

A musical score gives us a fascinating parallel to our life rhythms. The composer Amadeus Mozart once stated, "The music is not in the notes but in the silence between them." Silence *between* the notes.

The rest is not there to give the musician a breather but is an unassuming rhythmic pause used to drive the music. It serves as a pause intended for expression and is crucial for the movement of the melody.

How could a rest, or a short pause, be similarly placed in your life?

Take a moment to pause or wait. A fresh idea or a new thought may arise in your mind. In the space of a heartbeat you could discern insight into the need of a family member, a solution to some obstacle, or an idea for some good deed to accomplish. In a flash, you may become aware of a wrong you could right, or see yourself in a whole new light!

I have never heard the audible voice of God, but I have felt his tug moving me to make certain choices. Whatever comes in the rest note can serve as a catalyst to drive the music of your life.

The Shepherd of your soul leads you to lie down in green pastures, beside quiet waters, in a peaceful place. If that isn't a serene thought, I don't know what is. He does this for you! And he does it for a reason—to restore, heal, and guide you. It doesn't have to be complicated. He uses this time of rest and stillness for you to reflect, away from the clutter and clatter of life, away from screen time and all your beckoning duties. When you breathe into God's rest, it's as if you invite him to step in and settle the choppy waters of your mind.

Spiritual rest is *vital* for soul health. Augustine, an early church theologian and philosopher, spoke of finding rest in God. "Thou hast formed us for thyself, and our hearts are restless till they find rest in thee.'" The language may seem antiquated but the meaning is still relevant. Our hearts will remain restless, unsettled, and stormy unless we make the effort to find this rest God has offered.

Inhale his peace and be aware that he is by your side to guide you. Pray now,

O God, settle my mind. Help me follow you to the still waters of reflection, to wait and listen for your gentle nudges. Thank you for the offer of sweet rest. Even on days when there is much to do, remind me of the ways I can find nuggets of peace and trust you to guide me. Amen.

Breathing Deeper

1. What is the best time of day for you to practice stillness? Where is the best place?
2. Being still doesn't mean not moving. As you contemplate the health of your soul, what areas are in need of some loving attention?
3. Becoming aware of your failings is exactly the right time to invite God in to ask him to restore and mend your broken places. Why is there no better time to call for help?

6

The Practice of Quietness

"We need to find God, and he cannot be found in noise and restlessness. God is the friend of silence. See how nature— trees, flowers, grass—grow in silence; see the stars, the moon and the sun, how they move in silence. We need silence to be able to touch souls."
—Mother Teresa

I WAS INTERESTED TO LEARN that those who record professional music let their ears "relax" in a soundproof room before they finalize a soundtrack. This recalibration of noise levels allows them to be better equipped to hear the faintest imperfection in a recording. Though most of us do not have a sound room, it underscores the value of quietness to help recalibrate our hearts with our heads.

When was the last time you "heard" quietness?

Try turning off devices, notifications, minimize interruptions, and find a quiet place to simply *be*. If this sounds impossible in your hectic household or busy schedule, close your eyes, *inhale*, and imagine yourself meandering through the dappled shade of tall trees, breathing in fresh air and releasing all your stress. Imagine a peaceful, unrushed moment, perhaps a light rain falling or soft music playing, and breathe in deeply to allow your shoulders, neck, and ears to relax.

As you quiet the clamor, you create space for thoughts about your soul's health. To attain downtime in your life takes determination, and yet when you make this effort, the results are much-needed tranquility.

Who doesn't long for that?

As I wrote this, I found one definition of *tranquility* that brought me to a screeching halt. Tranquility is "an absence of demand and no pressure to do." I rolled my eyes. Seriously? Who lives on that planet? No pressure to *do*? That certainly doesn't sound like my life. So, I dug deeper into the meaning and thankfully found an additional description that seems a little more attainable: "the absence of disturbance or agitation, a feeling of calm. A disposition free from stress." This is the aim of quietness.

It is your soul's chance to recalibrate.

The Ever-Present Checklist

Some of us cling to our checklists like lint on a wool sweater. We falsely believe that if we check off all the items on our to-do list we will find satisfaction. But typically, at the end of a long day, even though we may feel a sense of accomplishment, there is always more that has been added to the list, and the reality of a tranquil moment has become a distant hope.

The compulsion of *doing* overrides *being*. There is a great temptation to allow our busyness to drive tranquil moments to the bottom of our list. Staying overly busy allows us to avoid going deeper and gives us
    perceived
        permission to
            procrastinate in our
                pursuit of soul health.

Consequently, when we don't first quietly consider our soul's disposition or seek God's thoughts for our day, we remain shallow with God and struggle mightily to find peace and quiet.

So, how do you push back from this table of chaos and fight for your spiritual well-being? It begins with a decision to spend time in quietness, to know that it is vital for spiritual growth and helps transform your soul. With less emphasis on doing, and more on being, your mind can loosen its vigilant need to protect, look more intently at today's life decisions, and set God's priorities for your day.

My hairstylist confided to me that she dreads any kind of quietness in her schedule since it forces her to reflect on unpleasant aspects of her life. Many of us carry a similar aversion to quiet moments and hope if we stay busy we might avoid the unpleasant bits. We fly through our days at breakneck speed, rarely taking time to reflect on deeper matters. With errands, projects, assignments, appointments, and endless to-do lists nipping at our heels, it's no wonder we feel hounded. But just because you continue to push uncomfortable realities away does not mean those troublesome areas will subside. I am confident I am not the only one who wants to pretend those areas dogging me aren't really a problem. We'd all rather look the other way.

If you must live by the checklist, you might add a bullet point to the top of your daily tasks: "Spend time being quiet!" Once you have it completed, you can strike through it with a flourish, then go off to conquer the day!

Consider this:

A life too busy becomes a life unexamined.
A life unexamined leads to fear of exposure.
A fear of exposure leads to shallow connections.
And shallow connections lead to loneliness.

Self-reflection and recalibration offer you depth and courage. They are well worth any effort you make. Developing the skill to be quiet and contemplative requires intention and energy in this noisy, bustling world.

Seeking Serenity

Ignatius of Loyola, a Jesuit Priest from the fifteenth century developed a prayer practice called the Examen. It was used to help children become more aware of the presence of God in their life and to recognize how he works in their days. It is a simple practice anyone can imitate as you quiet your mind and think about these four ideas:

1. Recall God's presence in your life,
2. Express gratitude,
3. Reflect on the day, and
4. Prepare for what lies ahead.

Following the pattern set forth in the Examen gives you a quiet moment to observe small glimpses of God in your life. You may sense his presence powerfully when you observe the intricacies of nature or when you are the recipient of kindness from a stranger. You may feel him through a meaningful conversation or even in an idea that pops up during prayer. The more you watch for God's presence, the more you realize he keeps showing up in your life.

In my efforts to hush my hectic pace, it sometimes helps me to think about what I would answer if God asked, "Where is your head today?" I might say, "My head is distracted and overwhelmed," or, "I'm tired." Perhaps I'd admit my worry about some circumstance looming on the horizon. Maybe

I'd give a cavalier response: "I'm good. Everything is under control. Now, let me get back to my list!"

An honest answer to such a question gives a clue as to where your head and your heart are in this moment. It is wise to face this question straight on and not simply flick it away like a pesky mosquito.

Once you learn the pattern of quietness, you will develop an uncanny ability to hear the distant drumbeat of your soul. You will gain a few precious moments with the God of eternity, a hushed respite to be soothed and reminded of his strength, a chance to contemplate his plan for giving you this particular day, and time to draw deep, calming breaths into your soul. It happens as you connect with your *authentic* self and find the best path forward. The writer of this Psalm gives us a beautiful vision of how this might look, "But I am calm and quiet. I am like a baby with its mother. I am at peace, like a baby with its mother" (Psalm 131:2, ICB).

A few moments of quietness help you plant your feet for the day, both for your benefit and the benefit of others. Another glance at the quote by Mother Teresa at the beginning of this chapter reminds us that "We need silence to be able to touch souls."

Ask the God of the universe to help you refrain from simply grinding through your checklist and live your life with his greater purpose in mind, touching each soul you encounter.

Searching for Solitude

The word *solitude* (to be alone and solitary) is easily understood yet challenging to attain because life is messy and noisy.

Jesus often took time for quietness and solitude. Imagine what it was to be him: People constantly clambering to be near you, to touch you, to be healed, to be fed; people questioning your motives, demanding answers; enemies looming; and even those close to you doubting and skeptical of your methods. Yes, he understood the value of time spent alone to gather his thoughts, and so, "Very early in the morning, while it was still dark, Jesus got up, left the house and went off to a solitary place where he prayed" (Mark 1:35).

You can find solitude and breathe in God's goodness whether walking alone or tucked under a blanket in your favorite chair. This time spent seeking quietness will give you a chance to think deeply and more comprehensively.

Susanna Wesley lived almost three hundred years ago and had ten (yes, ten!) children. Quiet and solitude would not come easily in that house. But not one to give up without a fight, Susanna had the quirky habit of pulling her apron up over her head as a signal to her children it was time for prayer, and she was not to be disturbed. In order to find some solitude with God, she blocked out the chaos, possibly the only way she could. Her sons, John and Charles Wesley, became influential theologians and writers of beautiful Christian hymns. As they told it, their spiritual impact was influenced greatly by their mother's dogged determination.

What life hacks can you utilize to deal with days that are jam packed? Between family demands, school events, and work agendas, it can be a fight to find time alone to think and pray. But rather than blithely ignoring your lack of solitude because it is so difficult to achieve, can you find small slivers of down time in order to refocus? Which "apron" can you throw over your head? (It is hard to imagine what my family would do if they came home and found me sitting with an apron over my head. This is the kind of behavior which only God could appreciate, but then, isn't that the point?)

Using strategies to benefit you both mentally and spiritually is vital. Here are a few perks to be enjoyed by carving out moments of solitude:

- You are able to ponder life decisions and reflect on goals and dreams.
- You are better able to articulate the pros and cons of choices ahead.
- You feel rejuvenated and clear minded.
- You've taken the time to think about areas that are troubling and pray for peace and help.
- You gain inspiration by spending time alone, perhaps out in nature or just under an apron somewhere.

In your quiet moments, welcome God's calming touch and hear him say, "Cease striving and know that I am God". (Psalm 46:10, LSB). God is bigger than any challenge you are facing, and he will help you gain a fresh perspective. Rest quietly in his presence and find the peace he promises. Draw in a long breath, release the muscles of your shoulders, and pray now:

God, quiet my heart and calm me as I throw my "apron" up over my head. Help me focus on the joys I gain in these moments of solitude. Remind me to watch for glimpses of you wherever I go and remember that you walk close to me. I know you have not called me to a life of busyness but to one of devotion. Please show me how to pry my hands from my ever-present to-do list so I can lift them to you. Deepen my breath and still my heart. Amen.

Breathing Deeper

1. Solitude is a time to welcome God's work in your life and to let him calm your heart. When and where do you find the best moments for solitude?
2. What does it mean for you to cease striving?
3. What would you answer if God asked you, "Where is your head today?"

7

The Art of Prayer

"Prayer is the opening of the heart to God as to a friend."
—Ellen White

WHEN WE PRAY, I WONDER if God hears our soul emit some low-frequency cry, like a mother hears and understands the inarticulate cries of her baby. Scripture is clear that one role of the Spirit is to make our needs known to God. "In the same way, the Spirit helps us in our weakness. We do not know what we ought to pray, but the Spirit himself intercedes for us through wordless groans" (Romans 8:26).

Have you ever felt that you wanted to pray but just didn't know what to say? This is not uncommon. Like a sigh too deep for words, we yearn to express to God what we feel but are not always able; our meager words won't surface, or we're unsure exactly what the burden is. This is when the spirit steps into the breach. *The Matthew Henry Bible Commentary* describes this *help* offered from the spirit with these words, God's spirit "heaves with us," as in, both sides lifting.[3] It is in that very moment the Spirit speaks words to God revealing what our soul longs to say.

The Spirit will intercede because God *wants* the relationship. He wants to be close to you and wants to hear from you. He has gone to great lengths to seek you out.

I appreciate this quote by Pastor Donald Whitney who said, "There is a psalm for every sigh of the soul." If you feel uncertain where to begin, you may wish to speak the psalms out loud to help get you started. Also, you can pray the Lords' Prayer or read aloud any prayers written in the Bible. Singing a song of worship to God is a prayer.

But mostly just speak what is on your heart. No eloquence or pattern is needed. God desires for you to communicate with him. The song, "Listen to our Hearts," by Steven Curtis Chapman, is a plea for God to hear what is in your heart on the days you can't find your own words to pray. God hears your heart. Your soul sings to him. So, when words are not enough, the deepest part of you is amazingly still able to convey your love for God. Don't give up! Keep praying. God is near.

A Whisper from God

A friend told me about a practice called the "listening prayer." Since it was a new concept to me, I gave it a try half hoping some cosmic voice would tell me the way to go. I sat quietly and asked God to show me what I needed to hear. I listened but got no message. At first, it produced a level of worry I wasn't doing something right, or perhaps God was disgruntled with my life and chose to remain distant. My friend reassured me, saying there is *not* a right way. We are simply striving to be receptors, to let him work in our life, to open our mind to him.

One day as I was contemplating my life, I heard, *I am responsible for my joy, I can't wait for it to come from other people.* This notion arrived on a day I struggled to be joy filled and wanted to blame others for the emptiness yawning in my heart. It wasn't an audible voice, but it came to mind from somewhere.

If we listen, what might we hear?

God speaks through His Spirit, which is alive in you, to move you forward in some way. When you take the time to be still and quiet the clatter, what might you hear? He can use any means to reach your heart, and it is his strong desire to do so.

No matter how God chooses to get our attention, we should welcome the ways he moves us. Some people are concerned about this concept of listening for God's voice, they are worried that people will hear only what they want to hear. Of course, this *could* happen, but if you are genuinely looking to find the way forward with your aim being a healthy, God-led soul, you can trust God to guide you.

A well-loved Proverb instructs us to, "Trust God from the bottom of your heart; don't try to figure out everything on your own. Listen for God's voice in everything you do, everywhere you go; he's the one who will keep you on track. Don't assume that you know it all. Run to God!" (Proverbs 3:5-6, MSG).

What is at the bottom of your heart? Trust God will find a way forward for you. Run to him! Listen for God's voice.

If you still feel uncertain about where to start, you might try the practice of "breath prayers." Speak a short verse or phrase, and hold it in focus as you breathe in. Here are some examples:

- "The Lord is my shepherd," hold this thought in your heart, think about it for a few beats, then exhale these words, "I shall not want" (Psalm 23:1, ESV). Wait a few moments and inhale the phrase again, "The Lord is my shepherd." Ponder what it means for your day; then exhale the second part again, "I shall not want."
- Breathe in, "My soul, find rest in God," then out, "My hope comes from Him" (Psalm 62:5). Repeat.
- Say the phrase, "Trust God from the bottom of your heart." Hold this thought; then breathe out, "Don't assume you know it all."

The more you breathe these truths, the more peace your heart will find. Focus-on your thought, allow it to wash over you and soothe your soul. This is God's promise to you, "Call to me and I will answer you and tell you great and unsearchable things you do not know" (Jeremiah 33:3).

Heaven Listens

In early biblical manuscripts, the Hebrew word for God is recorded as YHWH, but since the English language requires the use of vowels, an "a" and "e" have been arbitrarily added to make the name YAHWEH (pronounced YA-WAY).

As Sandra Thurman Caporale studied material from scholars and rabbis, a light went on in her head about the name of God. She discovered the letters YH and WH, when pronounced correctly, actually sound like breathing or aspirated consonants. (YH mimics the inhale and WH the exhale).

Her conclusions are astounding: As a baby our very first breath speaks the name of God and then throughout all our days, with every breath, every sigh, we call out the name of God. And then with our final breath, we leave this earth calling on the name of God.

Caporale concluded her article with this amazing thought, "God chose to give Himself a name that we can't help but speak every moment we're alive: All of us, all the time, everywhere; waking, sleeping, breathing, with the name of God on our lips."[4]

Prayer is as simple as breathing.

Your soul has a voice that heaven hears.

This psalmist declares, "He heard me from heaven; my cry reached his ears" (Psalm 18:6, TLB). What a thought! What you articulate in prayer reaches God's ears!

Pause now, breathe in, YH, breathe out, WH, and call to God from your heart.

O God, thank you that my soul's voice reaches your ears and that every breath I take calls to you. Speak truth and light into my soul today and draw me closer to your heart. Move my heart to a place where your voice will reach me. Thank you, Spirit, for heaving with me, for sharing my journey, and helping me to pray. Amen.

Breathing Deeper

1. To what lengths has God gone to have a close relationship with you?
2. What areas of your life bring God joy when he looks at you? Which areas does he see that need some loving attention?
3. Look again at Proverbs 3:5-6, "Trust God from the bottom of your heart." Name one area where you really need to trust God from the bottom of your heart.

PART THREE

Wounded Soul

EVERY SCAR TELLS A STORY.

I am sure the scar on the back of my leg was caused by the sharp teeth of an alligator partially submerged in the creek behind my childhood home. With the vivid imagination of a ten-year-old, I shrieked when I spotted the "creature" and ran full throttle for home! Keep in mind this was Colorado, and there are *no* alligators living there. More than likely, the gash on my leg came as I hit a sharp rock or a piece of glass in my terrified flight out of there. I can look back and laugh about it now. But some wounds, whether spiritual or emotional, cannot be laughed off so easily. Some wounds are acute and require serious attention.

Not all damage is equal. Stumbling down the stairs in public, may lead to physical pain, and more than likely deliver a blow to your pride. At some point, you could look back on it and chuckle at the memory of your misstep. But if you were pushed down the stairs by someone you thought you could trust, the experience would leave an altogether different mark on your soul. This type of betrayal is no laughing matter. We all have scars, and *everyone* understands what it is to be hurt. Everyone has been injured in life. Some injuries are minor or irritating, but others are major, causing significant and extensive distress.

Soul injury can leave you gasping for breath. Its damage comes in many shapes and sizes. Some memories are so painful to revisit or scary to relive that sometimes we would rather ignore, whitewash, or suppress the awful ache. But here is a certainty: stuffing soul injuries or "sweeping them under the rug" only prolongs the pain, and it *never* helps you heal.

A physical wound requires immediate cleansing and bandaging to prevent infection and give it the best chance to heal. In the same way, a spiritual wound should be attended to immediately, so it won't cause corrosion, bitterness, or scarring.

Likewise, older physical wounds that are thickened and leathered will benefit from treatments such as massage to help restore blood flow, special oils to soften the toughness, or possibly surgery to cut out the offensive scar tissue. Spiritual wounds from long ago that have turned into scars need a special touch—personal reflection, patience, openness, and prayer. Professional assistance may be required to work through certain types of damage and to find healing.

Some of the deepest scars are produced in some of the most private episodes. My friend suffered in silence for many years with her regret about a decision to have an abortion. She held the burden of this secret tightly in her heart. When she finally shared her story with a trusted friend, it brought about surprising relief and a chance to let the wound begin to heal. It didn't eradicate her regret, but it did help her feel liberated from hiding in the shadows and to find support from others who had similar scars.

To breathe life into your wounded soul, you must address the scars and gaping wounds. The path to healing may not be quick; it may not feel pleasant, but facing your injury is the right thing to do if you want to stop walking this earth as a wounded soul.

Does the healing of such wounds in your soul seem insurmountable? Does the idea of reliving an old injury stir up a heap of angst? I remember a troublesome conversation that occurred years ago that still causes my shoulders to tighten and my heart rate to increase. An insensitive comment was made that wounded a soul and ended a friendship. Such recollections can stir turbulent emotions because the memory remains, as does the pain.

In the next section, we will look at a number of approaches toward healing the wounds we have sustained, keeping in mind our goal of developing a beautiful soul.

Certainly, some wounds are perpetrated against us, while other injuries are inflicted *by us*. It is helpful to recognize the root of an injury and even learn to take responsibility for the parts we have brought on by our own actions. As stated earlier, damage comes in many shapes and sizes.

Review this table to consider a few general ways in which souls get damaged:

Soul Damage from Without	**Soul Damage from Within**
Spiritual Injury	
Harm occurs in religious circles, in the name of religion. It may have been caused by an esteemed church leader or fellow believer(s) with whom you've worshiped. Injuries in this realm can confuse or distort your faith.	Damage can occur when you believe God has allowed some painful circumstances in your life, or hasn't intervened when you thought he should. It can cause a crisis of faith or debilitating doubt. Resentment and disillusionment grow here.

Soul Damage from Without	Soul Damage from Within
Word and Deeds	
Wounds or harmful actions inflicted by others can cause significant pain in your soul. The harm is done, there is no do-over, and you face the huge task of trying to heal. At times it may feel lonely, unfair, or discouraging.	*You* said or did something that has resulted in negative consequences. When missteps and failures haunt you or harmful habits break your will, finding soul health requires resolve and intention.
Life's Circumstances	
Difficult situations—an illness, poverty, an accident, or death—occur; no one is immune. Even though it is not caused by you or someone, it still hurts in your soul.	Frequent complaining, pessimism, worry, or negative self-talk can hamper your spiritual progress. Damage happens when you accept flawed logic or misguided lies about yourself.

Take courage, soul health is less about you being *scarless* and more about you learning to honestly face your wounds to find peace of mind and a path to spiritual health.

Also, though it seems obvious, pray about the wound and let God in on your struggle. Let him know when you are afraid or angry or hesitant. As you approach any soul injury, cling to this promise, "[God] heals the wounds of every shattered heart. He sets his stars in place, calling them all by their names. How great is our God! There is absolutely nothing his power cannot accomplish, and he has an infinite understanding of everything" (Psalm 147:3-5, TPT). Wow! Everything. If he knows the name of every star, he knows every wound and every way you feel shattered. Stop for a moment and let this thought soothe you. Let it strengthen you.

Hope for Healing

Keep in mind, the goal of a healthy soul is not to diminish what you've been through or even erase your memories of the situation, but to help ease the pain over time as you gain a better perspective of it. The key to healing begins with your readiness to do some work on the issues, such as facing the wound, considering it from all angles, practicing forgiveness, learning openness, and reframing the situation from a spiritual standpoint.

Feeling nervous, uncertain, or cautious is normal when dealing with soul tenderness. But when disorienting emotions begin to circle, don't give up and decide it is useless or just too hard. Use the thoughts to reveal what might be holding you back. When a fearful thought arises, let it remind you to go deeper.

Instead of letting the injury define who you are (rejected, abused, mistreated, judged), picture yourself instead growing, deepening, healing, and making strides toward spiritual stability. Can you see it?

The following questions may help you gain fresh perspective on a challenging circumstance:

- Do you need a new viewpoint? Is your vantage point too narrow? Too broad?
- Is there something here for you to learn? What is God trying to teach you?
- Do you need to make a decision? What choices can you make today to lead to healing?

- Do you need to set up protections? What is the best way to guard your soul from future wounds?
- Who can relate to what you are going through? Who do you know who has healed—or helps people heal—in circumstances similar to yours? How and when can you reach out?
- What framework is available to support you? Where can you find your best support?
- Is there a relationship that needs your attention? Is there someone to whom you should apologize? Is there someone you need to forgive?
- How can you be more transparent? How can you allow more light to shine on your fear, pain, or shame?
- Is your security an issue? Do you need to find a safer environment?
- What role does timing play? Are you going to keep putting this off, or are you ready to pursue healing now?

Breathe deeply and pray for healing to unfold gently, like a tree unfurling its leaves in the springtime, reaching toward the sky. As you do the outstanding work of soul care, sprouts of spiritual health will most certainly emerge.

The deepest healing of a soul will come in waves, never all at once. No one easily measures progress in the center of a storm. Be gentle, suspend harsh judgment of yourself, and quiet your insecurities. Strive for patience as you heal. Take a step forward, then live in that space for a time, adapt to the *new* you until you are ready to move forward again.

In the 1950s and '60s, a time of deep wounds in the US, minister and social activist Martin Luther King Jr. rallied his supporters, encouraging them to persevere in the battle for justice. He exclaimed, "If you can't fly, run. If you can't run, walk. If you can't walk, crawl. But by all means keep moving!"

Even if you are barely crawling, go at whatever pace you need. Don't feel you must address everything today. Don't expect to heal by *yourself*. Healing in your soul comes from reliance on God and others as well as doing the work within yourself.

Please persist. Do anything but remain stuck in your pain.

Even when that pain tries to pinch your heart shut, move yourself forward somehow. Understand that building soul health will sometimes require a Herculean effort. Pray and ask God for the fortitude to carry on. He has promised to stay by your side and heal the pierced places in your soul.

Even if you feel as though you are barely holding it together, remember, you are not alone. There are others facing similar struggles. Together with them, you can make this journey. And never forget, God remains near to you.

8

How Do I Face My Scars?

"Out of suffering have emerged the strongest souls; the most massive characters are seared with scars."
—Kahlil Gibran

WHILE SOME PEOPLE HAVE ONLY a scant interest, many are deeply intrigued with the British royalty, enjoying their traditions, pageantry, and those marvelous hats. They buy magazines with their scandals splashed across the covers and consume shows detailing the adventures of the royally rich and genetically fortunate.

It sparked my interest when I read about the wedding gown of Princess Eugenie. The front of the dress was perfectly coiffed, as we'd expect for a princess, yet from behind, the plunging back of the dress unexpectedly revealed a long, deep scar. According to the reports, as a young girl, she suffered from Scoliosis and had to have numerous surgeries to correct her spine.

Why would any bride want to expose something so dreadful?

When questioned by reporters, the princess said she chose the low-cut back because it was "a lovely way to honor those who cared for me and to give courage to those who also suffer."

Wow! What a noble gesture! Her action impacted many because she readily shared her scar; she didn't hide or downplay it.

When You Hide Your Scars

Anyone who has more than a little time on this earth will have blemishes and scars, whether visible or buried out of sight. We choose to hide them for many reasons. Exposing our scars is often painful and we may feel ashamed or afraid to allow others to see how we've been injured.

Although it is human nature to hide our broken parts, here's what I've discovered: when I avoid being transparent about my difficulties, when I attempt to limit my exposure, I only end up blocking people out of my life. The end result only adds more distress to my existing ache. I become:

- Isolated and lonely since no one knows the real me.
- Irrational, believing (falsely) if others knew the truth about me, they would freak out.
- Insecure, when I accept the lie that I must be the only person who is so broken.

Why do I do this? Why does anyone? The reasons are legion: self-protection against the judgment of others, worry of being unfairly criticized, fear of more pain, dread of reliving a tough memory, uncertainty of what is really going on inside, to name a few.

Your efforts to keep the injury under wraps only hurts you in the long run. An unshared injury will not heal because when your thoughts get discombobulated, common sense is pushed out of the equation. Acknowledging your wounds and scars is a first step to achieve soul healing. Dare to tell your story to a trustworthy, praying person.

Princess Eugenie exposed her scar not to elicit pity but to give others hope for their own journey. As you open yourself up about your troubles, you will inspire others to make similar bold steps.

In numerous conversations over the years, people have shared their agony with me about harm done to them. Their injuries, whether inflicted intentionally or by accident, by someone else or by themselves, fill every crevice of their heart like an icy winter storm. The chill goes bone deep and numbs the soul, leaving a wide spectrum of damage, such as mangled emotions, bodily harm, disappointment, heartbreak, conflict, and loss. The wounds cripple us all in some way and leave tender scars.

Whatever damage has been done to your soul is your scar to bear. Comparing whose damage is worse is counterproductive. But in the same way that everyone experiences injury, everyone can lean in to help others who are also hurting. Sometimes it helps to remember that God understands your scars. As the old hymn says:

"I am headed for a home built by God alone . . .
Where the only thing there made by man
Are the scars in the hands of Jesus."[5]

The only human-made item in heaven is a scar.
God understands scars.

When Scars Skew Your Vision

Have you heard the story about the woman who criticized a neighbor for hanging dirty clothes out on her clothesline? One day the woman's husband observed how filthy their windows were, and she suddenly realized the stains she saw on her neighbor's laundry were from her own dirty windows!

Sometimes your window of life gets dirty or is defined by what happened in your past. Your story of injury can easily become the filter through which you view all other circumstances. Are you letting that narrative influence your everyday life—every discussion and every decision? If this is your tendency, your wounds will remain tender, unhealed, and in danger of worsening.

Washing your window of life could be as simple as:

- Taking the time to look more deeply into your own heart.
- Searching for another perspective to the situation.
- Exchanging a negative thought with a positive one.
- Working through an issue of forgiveness.
- Getting to know the other person more deeply.
- Opening your heart to a trusted source.
- Scheduling an appointment with a professional therapist.

Any positive step you take to renew your *view* allows the wounds to begin to heal. Remember, you are a work in progress. Be gentle with yourself as you face your scars.

When Scars Slow Your Journey

Many people experience a wild swing of emotions when they deal with their wounds, much like being on a giant swing. We soar up into the trees of denial, trying to feel nothing about our injury; then reality sets in and down we go toward the pain and misery before going right back up again bemoaning the fact that we are hurt. We know in our heads that we should attempt to find some semblance of balance between the extreme emotions, but it is hard to know where to begin.

If you have a scar that needs to be healed but are unsure how to begin, start by asking yourself some of these straightforward questions. Your answers will help you understand how you can make progress in your soul's health.

- Are you trying to control the matter and make it go *your* way? Are you so determined to get a certain outcome that you are not open to a different approach?
- Are you trying to change others to think like you do? Do you reject or disapprove of them when they do not?
- Are you quick to defend your actions? In what ways are you justifying your behavior? Are you unwilling to hear other viewpoints?
- Are you afraid? If so, what are you afraid of?
- Are you worried? If so, what specifically worries you?
- Are you angry? If so, what particularly makes you angry about the situation?
- Because of the hurt have you withdrawn your heart and run away? Are you pouting in a pity party? Are you down on yourself, casting dispersion on current or past failures?
- Are you on the offensive, lashing out like a wounded tiger, or using sharp words? Are you slandering, criticizing, or blaming the people or person who hurt you? Are you trying to get even?
- Are you blowing off the incident or convincing yourself it's *their* problem and they need to deal with it?

Make every effort to answer these questions honestly, always aiming for truth in your soul.

Take a moment now to ask God to help you heal from your wounds. As you consider the spiritual health you desire, pray these words:

O my God, you understand scars! Thank you for being relatable to me in this way. Reach for me on the days my pain is so great, and I can't find a way to reach for you. Flood my dark days with your light and love and unbind my sorrow. Show me where my "windows" are dirty; help me clear my view. Help me resolve what I can, so I can treat people with your grace. Amen.

Breathing Deeper

1. What are you learning about the current condition of your soul? What is God teaching you?
2. About which areas do you avoid transparency? Have you pulled back your heart from others? In which ways are your actions causing you to be lonely and insecure?
3. In what way is your window of life dirty? How should you clean it?

9

I Am Not Alone

"Faith is a way of waiting—never quite knowing, never quite hearing or seeing, because in the darkness we are all but a little lost."
—Frederick Buechner

SOMETIMES, WOUNDS INFLICTED BY OTHERS will impact your belief system. As a result, you may experience disillusionment, bitterness, disappointment, and doubt. You might even distance yourself from God or abandon faith altogether.

When Faith Fractures

Growing up, Doreen had no spiritual influence from her dysfunctional family and knew very little about Christianity except what she heard from friends or saw on TV. While in college, she met a group of exuberant Christians who poured love and kindness into her life, and she was awed by the sense of belonging she felt. After several months, she became a follower of Jesus, and her newfound faith filled every empty part of her.

Years later, the dynamic group began to implode due to disunity, deceit, and arrogance. The ugliness of it crushed Doreen's faith and left her disillusioned. With no other religious experience to compare it to, she felt as if her spiritual family was shattering. The ordeal broke her trust in the people she thought were devoted to God, the people she had looked to and emulated. It brought her spiritual journey to a limping halt.

As she told me about her experience, I felt an ache of helplessness to ease her sadness. What could I say to counter the bad behavior of men and women who should have known better? I reminded her (and myself) that God is bigger than any mistakes made by people; he's bigger than her broken heart. In order to mend, we must accept what has happened, learn from it, and keep in mind that God knows what is going on.

The somber truth is that too many people have experienced harm in the name of religion. Part of Doreen's spiritual injury was meted out by those with religious authority. When such people mistreat or abuse our trust, it is disorienting because they aren't who we thought they were, and they aren't acting like a spiritual person should act. We feel disillusioned, and it leaves a mark—one with which we must contend if we hope for healing and an ongoing relationship with God.

Don't be surprised if when dealing with a deep wound it will take more than one try to release the pain. In his book *Lighter*, author Yung Pueblo writes, "If the pain was deep you will have to let it go – many times."[6] It isn't a one and done process. It will take some finessing and new approaches, as well as many re-starts and fresh tries.

When Expectations Fall Short

In addition, your soul may feel injured when your expectations of God are different from your reality. Do you think God should be doing more to help, or overall do you feel disappointment with unanswered prayers? Perhaps you believe God has abandoned you in your darkest hour.

Maybe you or someone you know is angry and bitter because God allowed something terrible to happen in their life. (Have you ever heard someone say, "A loving God wouldn't have allowed this to happen!"?) It is easy to want to blame God when some part of life breaks.

When trouble strikes our first thought is often, "Why is this happening? Why me?" Since such questions can never be answered, perhaps we should ask more helpful questions, ones that *can* be answered, such as: "What can I learn from this challenge?" or "How is this pain leading me to more depth in my faith." Or you might ask, "How will I gain more relatability to others who struggle?"

Those who grapple with their wounds and strive to learn are capable of great empathy toward fellow sojourners. Tough challenges can also help burn away our pettiness, short-sightedness, or self-centeredness, and force us to dig deeper to find the good in the situation.

Maybe you feel like there is nothing to learn; it is simply hard. That is okay too. Even when a soul gets shattered into tiny pieces, and it feels like all the shards are only fit to be swept into a dustpan, God knows where each piece of you is. He carefully takes those splintered bits and kindly sets out to restore your beautiful soul and help you breathe again. He is gentle, like a parent holding a newborn, whispering soft, soothing tones of love over you.

Trusting him with these tender places isn't a magic formula. It doesn't guarantee you won't have pain nor does leaning into his kindness erase the hurt. He remains close in your pain, disappointment, and struggle and reminds you that pain and joy can exist in the same life. God sees your wounds, and he cares.

Consider this poignant thought by Viktor Frankl, a twentieth-century psychiatrist and Holocaust survivor: "What is to give light must endure burning." If you want light, something must burn. Though you may never understand why God allows the shattering, you can be sure there is some light, some good that will come out of your heartache. Rather than blaming God for everything that is wrong, imagine what beauty he will create from the ashes.

The Truth about Doubt

When your wounded soul causes you to *doubt* God's care or interest in your life, you might feel conflicted or guilty. But is it wrong to doubt?

In his book *A Christian Survival Guide* Ed Cyzewski wrote, "Jesus wouldn't have had a single follower if doubt disqualified anyone from following him."[7] Even though Jesus taught that we should believe, doubt itself doesn't shut us out from pleasing God.

Doubt always treads on the heels of belief, so don't be surprised when it trips you up as you aspire for a beautiful, healthy soul.

Many biblical characters had periods of hesitation and fear. If we disregarded all who had misgivings and doubt, the Bible would be extremely short! Jesus was patient with those who were uncertain.

As a young believer, Carol grappled with the viability of the miracles she read about in the Bible and by extension was doubting her faith. She sought out a spiritual director who, at first, earnestly tried to help her through reasoning, archaeological proofs, and personal anecdotes. After a few months, with Carol still struggling, the exasperated director told her, "It's right there in the Bible. If you cannot accept it, why do you keep coming back?"

His impatience and lack of compassion for her genuine conflicts brought Carol's pursuit to an abrupt stop. I wonder sometimes what might have been different in Carol's faith journey if the director had shown more mercy, patience, and Christlikeness. If we give people the space and time to work through their questions, how many might find their way back to God?

I have personally been on both sides of this "courtroom drama." In some instances, I have been the judgmental one, looking down my long spiritual nose at those who doubted, believing they should "get it together" and just get over their questioning. At other times, I stood at the "mercy of the court," doubting and wrestling with my own beliefs, only to find myself on the receiving end of judgment and condescension. Such treatment never helped me navigate through my weeds of doubt. God is a God of mercy; we should all strive to be more like him!

The truth is, doubt or the deconstructing of one's faith does *not* disqualify you from following God. Our effort means something to God. Thomas Merton, a theologian from the early twentieth century wrote this prayer: "I believe the desire to please you, does in fact please you." This helps me find peace in times of uncertainty.

Even in the midst of doubt, we can grow and evolve in our belief, allowing our close examination and questions to serve us well. While doubting is certainly not an ideal place to remain, we can and should make room for it. Here are some truths about doubt:

- Doubt doesn't erase your faith. It may cause you to hesitate or hold back a little, but the tension between doubt and faith can promote spiritual growth.

- Doubt is beneficial when it challenges the status quo. It helps you reflect on what you believe, pushes you to search deeper, makes your faith stronger and it becomes your own.
- Doubt can lead you to ask profound questions and to seek deeper answers.

To deal better with doubt, let God in on it. Don't ignore God because doubts are present. Let him be a part of your steps to building faith. Tell him about your difficulties, express your frustration with Christians who don't walk the talk and be honest about scriptures you find problematic. It's nothing he hasn't heard before.

Think about God thinking about you.

Doubt is not the end of your story. God's love for you *is* the story! Cling to this morsel of hope, this tiny mustard seed of faith; that's all it takes to overcome a whole lot of doubt. The truth is, you don't have to have every answer figured out to believe God has a role in your life.

Release the tension of doubt wedged deep between your shoulder blades. Breathe in and pray this now:

God, you are good to me. Thank you for your patience in my times of doubt and for letting me question and figure out this journey. Sometimes faith is confusing, and I feel unsure if I can stay. But you always stay, and for that I am grateful. When you expose the fissures in my soul, remind me you are close by to help me grow and change. Give me genuine readiness to face the pieces of my heart I'd rather hide. Help me to be gracious toward those who doubt and be patient when they struggle. Amen.

Breathing Deeper

1. "God is bigger than any mistakes made by me or by people." How does this idea speak to my heart?
2. In what ways is my faith being tested? How are my doubts refining my beliefs?
3. In what ways do I look down on people who believe differently than me? How can I practice more grace?

10

Rising From the Ashes

"There are wounds that never show on the body that are deeper and more hurtful than anything that bleeds."
—Laurel K. Hamilton

SOUL INJURY IS PAINFUL. WHEN you have been flattened by pain, recovery can feel impossible, like trying to unscramble an egg.

You might ask, "How do I come back from such damage?" Words like these have been spoken by anyone who has ever breathed on this planet. Not one of us hasn't felt the crush of devastation.

Wounds inflicted on us by others can cause significant pain to our soul. When people disappoint us, hurt us, or mistreat us in some way, it undermines trust; our feelings get stung, and our confidence is shaken. Like a wrecking ball, the negative actions—bullying, neglect, criticism, ill-treatment, ingratitude, sarcasm, or gossip—all of them crash into and shatter the heart.

The concept of rising from ashes originates in ancient Egyptian folklore about the mythical phoenix. It was believed that this fanciful bird with its fiery red plumage symbolized hope for a *new life*. As the story goes, with a lifespan of up to five hundred years, there could only be one bird living at any time. Just before its life was up, the bird would build a nest and set itself on fire allowing the new phoenix to rise from the ashes. Like this fictional bird, we too can emerge from any disaster stronger, smarter, and restored to face another day.

Borrowing from this idea, we will look closely at our soul injury and assess the damage done, reconsider how we react, find use for our pain, and, in short, rise up stronger than before.

Assess the Damage

One woman, attempting to turn left onto a busy road after looking both ways, was struck by a motorcyclist she had not seen. There was a terrible crunching sound of metal on metal as the motorcycle stopped but the rider did not. She was horrified as the rider flew across her windshield as if in slow-motion. With a swift shot of adrenaline, she pulled her car to the side of the road and ran to the young man lying crumpled on the ground.

Her immediate thought was to assess how badly he was hurt. He was breathing, thank goodness, but was in obvious pain. Other drivers had stopped, and she shouted out, "Call 911!" Once emergency services were on the way, there was nothing else she could do but sit, hold his hand, and try to soothe him until they arrived.

Soul wounds can be every bit as severe. When your soul has been wounded, you must first assess the damage to determine the severity of the injury. It may feel like you have flown over the proverbial windshield of a car or maybe you are just a little bruised. This time of evaluation will help you make vital steps toward recovery. Rather than block your hurt feelings or lash out to hurt others, focus on taking long deep breaths. Move slowly as you allow you emotions to settle and pray for clarity about the injury.

Once the damage has been done, it is still important to stop and consider these few checkpoints. They will help you attain soul health more readily. Once you have ascertained the condition of your soul, use the following list of questions to help you to regain your spiritual footing:

- Is it possible that you may be misinterpreting the actions or words of the one who hurt you?
- Do you have unrealistic expectations?
- Is there something that may be happening or has happened in their life to prompt their behavior?
- What, if anything, did you do or say to provoke the action? (Of course, it may not be you at all, but it *is* a fair question. It is always helpful to examine your own behavior.)
- Did this situation trigger a severe response due to long-ago, stuffed-away hurts? Or might your strong reaction be coming from troubles brewing in an altogether different corner of your life?
- Is this someone with whom you need to remain connected, or should you put some space between you for a time? Obviously, choose wisely how to proceed when considering family members, coworkers, or neighbors.

Framing Your Reactions

Consider how you might take an alternate look at your soul's injury. It will help to remember your goal is to maintain a healthy soul! Try to focus on your own responses and not the behavior of others. Consider compassion and patience. Accept that God knows what happened and that he remains right beside you and wants to help you heal.

One day my boss sent an email saying he'd like to see me. I immediately felt nervous, wondering what I had done to prompt his message. My anxiety grew. I knew I had been a little distracted since my mom got sick, but I was certain my work had not suffered. *How did he have the nerve to call me in after I had worked so hard?* Insecurity and worry were popping in my head like Pop Rocks candy.

Feeling somewhat jittery, I took a deep breath and walked into his office. "You wanted to see me?"

"Hey Janet, I know work has been crazy, and you've been under a lot of pressure with your mom being so sick. I've noticed the extra hours you've put in and wanted to suggest you take a couple days and get some time away from the office."

Well! Color me embarrassed! Here I was assuming the worst when he was simply looking out for me. Red in the face, I thanked him for his thoughtfulness and trudged back to my office, wondering about my rash reaction. How easy it is to get sideways with someone by reacting to a false set of assumptions. The extreme reaction to my boss was not warranted, yet hurts from previous heavy-handed, unkind authority figures surged from their hiding places. My first inclination was to give my fear full rein. Here is an unsettling thought I once heard: "Unaddressed emotions don't mind being suppressed, they simply head down to the basement of your heart and lift weights." Wow! This idea makes me want to rethink how I manage my injuries! It never helps to suppress our negative emotions.

Injuries will come. How you respond is important, but keep in mind, your first reaction is just that, a reaction. Give yourself a minute to decide the best way to reply. Step back and assess the situation and then you can best choose how you will respond. Spiritual healing comes when you bid farewell to simply reacting, and instead examine the circumstance from all angles to get a better viewpoint. Your emotions may come along for the ride, but as a passenger not the driver!

Look over these questions as you reframe your spiritual outlook:

- What brings you joy? Can you place your focus there instead of perseverating on the injury?
- Can you treat others the way you want to be treated even if they don't honor you with the same kind of behavior? (Remember, you can't change anyone other than yourself.)
- Will you avoid this person or walk on eggshells around them?
- Can you find a path to maneuver around or beyond the hurt to find true joy and live your life in peace?
- Is your lens of pain or disappointment making you unable to see all sides?

Wounded Healers

How can you overcome your difficulties? Is there some way to turn them and make them useful? In her book *Wholehearted Faith* author Rachel Held Evans writes, "[God] comes alongside us when we go through hard times, and before you know it, he brings us alongside someone else who is going through tough circumstances similar to ours."[8]

You are able to redeem your pain when you allow God to comfort you, embolden you, and equip you to help others. Consider the following examples of people who are doing so:

- A mother whose teenage son took his own life leads a suicide prevention campaign across the nation to address mental health, depression, and bullying.

- A woman, sexually abused by a church leader writes books about overcoming and helps others find their voice to speak out and speak up.
- A man whose father died of ALS participates in fundraisers each year by riding his bike hundreds of miles to raise awareness and funding to support research.
- A woman who battles with loneliness and fear writes three encouraging cards each week to widows in her church. Perhaps a small token, but those on the receiving end see it differently!
- An elderly woman who experienced extreme poverty (and cold) when her daughter was born built a team of knitters who knit tiny caps for preemie babies at the hospital where her daughter now works as a nurse.
- A marriage that fell apart due to unfaithfulness left both spouses feeling little hope. Through hours of counseling, repentance, and forgiveness, their marriage has been restored, and they strive to help other couples in similar struggles.

I call these compassionate people "wounded healers." When you have endured soul-splitting injury, finding purpose in the pain is your best bet to overcome. When advocating for others, remind them they are not alone and walk by their side. It won't erase what you've endured, but God uses it to help heal *your* heart.

The way one friend tells it, she doesn't want to waste even one ounce of the pain she has experienced nor forget the valuable lessons she has learned. I've known her for years and can tell you she has a lot of reasons to blame, accuse, and stomp her foot. Victimized by a stepparent the first half of her life then ground down by a spouse with mental illness the second half, she's got a lot of forgiving to do. This woman is tenacious and refuses to go under; she works to exchange her heartache for insight, wisdom, and compassion. She has had sessions with professional therapists, hefty discussions with friends and mentors, and long walks pleading to God for relief. Success means daily decisions to release the stranglehold of bitterness about life's unfairness. Her focus is on the good in her life and on what possibilities lie before her. One of her great joys is to help others who are hurting to find morsels of good buried in the rubble. She is a "wounded healer".

Contemplate these questions to find ways you can help others with your experiences:

- Who do you know who might benefit from what you've experienced?
- What part of your difficult circumstance might offer faith to people who need a hand up?
- How could your injury be turned into something useful?

To become a wounded healer, first you must have a heart to help others understand they are not alone. Keep in mind it is not your job to carry their burden, nor should you dump all your woes on them as you relate to their journey. Simply allow your ordeal to be a light, to show them they are seen and understood.

One woman who was deeply discouraged from a long period of sickness questioned why God even kept her alive. Her companion replied, "As long as you have breath, there is someone who needs what you have to offer." Such amazing advice! Despite your pain, mistakes, or disappointments, as long as you have breath, there is more you can give to others.

Helping someone else does not mean you are "over it" or don't still feel the pain. But you harness the ache in your soul for a life of purpose. Can you wrap your mind around the idea that as long as you are still here, you are useful? Assess the damage, decide to forgive, and become a wounded healer. It is just one useful tool to help you recover and rise from the ashes.

Give it a chance. Look for those who might benefit from what you offer, use your experiences to help them, and see what God will do with the breath still in you as you pray this now:

Oh, my God, take the breath I still have and help me use it well. Fill my lungs with life and hope. Help me remember I matter to you. I long to redeem my pain by helping others to be patient and to rise from the ashes as you shine your light in my life once more. Teach me to release anger and retaliation and forgive as you do. Thank you for redeeming my life. Amen.

Breathing Deeper

1. In which areas of your life do you need to practice self-forgiveness?
2. What are the unaddressed emotions hiding in your "basement"? Why do you allow them to remain in hiding? What might occur if you shared them with a trusted friend?
3. How can you redeem your difficulty and help others by becoming a wounded healer?

Please note, if you are experiencing any sort of physical or emotional abuse, seek help immediately. Schedule an appointment with a licensed therapist, call a hotline, or talk to a trusted friend.

11

Surrendered Soul

"Nothing will ever change while you point the finger of blame. Out of responsibility comes possibility."
—Lisa Villa Prosen

GOD NEVER WASTES A DROP of your tears.

He uses what you endure to mold and build your character; he takes your faults and blunders and then shapes them, scuffs and all, into something beautiful. He sees you as his divine creation and longs to fill you with peace and overflowing joy.

David, the long-ago king of Israel, is described in Scripture as a "man after [God's] own heart" (1 Samuel 13:14). This depiction is amazing, since David had deceived those close to him, committed adultery, and was guilty of murder. But he was also a father who lost an infant to death and a grown son to a national rebellion. His earnest dream of building a temple for God was given to another. His wife mocked him publicly and rejected him. As a young man, anointed by God's prophet to be the next king, he was pursued relentlessly for years by the jealous current king who wanted to kill him.

Talk about wounds.

David loved God. You love God. Like you, there were days when he didn't do the right thing. On one of those dark days, it took another prophet sent by God to press home the poignant truth that David had drifted far away from where he should be.

The powerful words of the prophet shook David to his soul and caused him to dig deep and look closely at his heart in order to regain his peace with God. David's moving prayer in Psalm 51 offers three practical steps for renewal:

1. David acknowledged, "For I know my transgressions, and my sin is always before me" (Psalm 51:3). When you admit your weak areas and allow God to shine a light on you, you become more aware of your soul condition. Your reactions, good or bad, demonstrate a lot about your soul's well-being.
2. His prayer continues, "Surely you desire truth in the inward parts. You teach me wisdom in the *inmost* place" (Psalm 51:6 WEB). A renewed soul springs from honesty and openness. This is God's desire for you, to bear truth inside. It led David to ask for a steadfast heart, one that would remain upright.
3. The prayer closes out as David asks God, "Restore to me the joy of your salvation and grant me a willing spirit, to sustain me." (Psalm 51:12). This request wasn't for only a one-time offer but for the blessing of joy sustained over time, and for salvation.

The hardships David faced humbled him and drove him to his knees. Yes, he made poor choices, experienced disappointment, and felt afraid, but eventually all of it pointed him back to God. His heart was softened, ready to learn and to grow.

Face the Truth

There is no shortage of pain any of us has inflicted directly on our own souls. Stupid decisions, regrettable actions, and flat-out failures form the base of the story we tell. Injury can cause pain long after the initial hurt has passed. Everyone makes missteps, feels remorse, and experiences miserable pangs of guilt, but when it lands on our doorstep, especially those self-inflicted injuries, it's tough to face. After the damage is done, we are left with regret racing around in our heads, rarely giving us a moment's peace. Detrimental decisions can haunt us and cause sleepless nights. We invariably wonder what might have happened if we'd handled it another way, made a better choice.

While it is easy to second guess yourself, all that is left to do is take responsibility for your actions. You must be intentional and look hard for ways to learn from the damage done. As you do, allow yourself large doses of mercy, self-forgiveness, kindness, and patience!

What hurts one person may not affect another. I learned this painful lesson when I thoughtlessly popped a friend of mine on the mouth because she would not stop teasing me.

She was furious!

We were at the park enjoying a beautiful Autumn day. A recent blunder I had made in front of a group of colleagues came up in the conversation. She began to poke fun at me about it not realizing that I felt embarrassed about my mistake. She thought it was humorous, but I wasn't amused. For me, it was just a casual tap on her lips to shush her, but for her it was the epitome of disrespect. I sincerely apologized, but it took a while for us to move past the emotion that jarred our relationship; I still cringe when I think about it.

It is tempting to finesse the narrative. The story I *want* to tell is that I meant no harm and that she overreacted. But the truth is somewhere closer to the middle, that we hurt each other and that we both made careless miscalculations. Both sides were in the wrong.

We stood, awkwardly in that gray puddle of ambiguity, faced with finding the balance between letting this incident dominate our friendship or pressing through the dodgy bits to rebuild our connection. The scar remains, as does the memory.

Some days when the memory surfaces, I shut down any negativity and say to myself, "Nope, not going there. We've dealt with this, and it's settled." Other days, when I am not paying attention to my soul's well-being, it takes only one small reminder to spiral me into a corkscrew of regret, which in turn impacts how I feel about myself, or how I treat others—all stemming from an incident that took place long ago.

Everyone makes bad choices and is tempted to try to stow them in a dark corner and hope they stay hidden. But realize, suppressing the emotions from those unfortunate scenarios wrecks any kind of soul building! The more you are willing to admit your mistakes, the better progress you will make toward spiritual growth. The more you embrace a tender heart, the more joy you will hold.

A Gift Called Forgiveness

Forgiving and forgetting is simply not realistic.

Yep, you read that right. You can't and you don't forget the ways you have been injured—and sharply recall the wrong done to you. The scars remain, and yet you are asked to somehow live on, bearing up under them. How can you forgive in the light of remembering?

Any journey to forgiveness will be fraught with challenges since the desire to retaliate, to "give as good as you get," is an extremely strong impulse. You may hesitate to forgive because you don't want to let someone off the hook. But ask yourself, will revenge ever help? Does mimicking someone's harmful actions bring about a desirable outcome? Does getting back at someone make anything better? Sure, it may feel satisfying for a few moments, until you realize you're right back where you started, still sitting in the pit of misery, robbed of genuine joy.

One of the sweetest women I know says, "Forgive and forget. If you can't forget, forgive each time you remember." Her obvious kindness touches my heart. The reality is this: When you make the *choice* to forgive, you will find unexpected gifts of peace, clarity, and the ability to breathe deeper. Anger, anxiety, and hostility dissipate and have no more hold on you. And to top it off, as you recognize the good choices you are making, you connect deeper with the Creator of your soul.

Forgiveness is a gift! A reward to your own soul.

An author once received numerous hateful emails assaulting her writing. The messages caused her severe waves of anger and hurt. One weekend, she and a friend decided to turn the negative vitriol into something positive. They printed copies of the terrible emails and folded each of them into a beautiful origami flower. As they did, they prayed for each individual who wrote them.

Sharing what she learned from the ordeal, Rachel Held Evans wrote in her book *Wholehearted Faith:* "I am a very real human being, living a very real life, with a very real capacity to be very hurt but also to be healed, to hate but also to love, to harm but also to forgive."[9] Clearly, negative words and actions can knock you down and suck the breath right out of your lungs, but the capacity to choose the better response is yours. You make the choice:

To be hurt or be healed,
To hate or to love,
To fume or to forgive.

The author demonstrated an impressive response to a difficult circumstance. Similarly, my nephew Chris holds to the mantra, "assume no malice." He generously gives the benefit of the doubt wherever he can. It is a choice; it's how he lives his life.

What a gift.

Sleepless Nights

Sometimes an injury is caused by another person, but our response to it amplifies the pain and inflicts self-injury.

I learned a lesson late one night as cords of anger tied a knot in my chest, twisting and turning me like ivy around a garden gate. I was unable to sleep as angry thoughts hummed through my mind. Someone I love had been deviously manipulated and mistreated, and her soul was badly injured. Though I had prayed numerous times and made attempts to forgive the person who had hurt her, the anger still scratched like sandpaper.

That night I couldn't ignore the injustice. Yes, this injury was initially caused by someone else, but because of my response to it, I faced a wound of my own doing. Such is the nature of dark, angry thoughts skulking in the shadows; they stand at the ready, waiting for moments of weariness. (And who doesn't circle the drain at such times?) As I storm-walked through the house that night, a verse popped into my head: "Search me O God and know *my* heart. Test me and know my anxious thoughts. See if there is any offensive way *in me* and lead me in the way everlasting" (Psalm 139:23-24, italics mine).

This verse, written centuries ago, forced me into a corner as I was pressed to ask where the "offensive way" placed its foot, at that person's door or mine. Certainly, there could be blame placed at the door of the one who hurt my friend, but my reactions of hatred, anger and bitterness, well those were all mine.

The writer of this scripture had a heart eager to please God. And, of course, I wanted such a heart, but standing in my kitchen that night, the truth came in an instant. I was justifying my hateful thoughts on the bad actions of another person, but was anyone (me included) helped by my anger and hopes for revenge? Clearly, my soul was in rough shape. I was in misery.

When your heart feels a tug, how willing are you to look further into the shadowy corners? Do you ask God to search you and show what is truly going on inside? Even if your initial response is to look away, what if, instead, you invited God to join you right in that vulnerable place? What if you made room for him to come in and offer reassuring places of peace?

Surely, there is no safer place to have your heart laid bare than before the one who created that very heart. Even though your thoughts are less than desirable, God will move you closer to his path of peace, if you will allow it.

Be the person who recognizes and admits the spiritual struggle against your wrong choices, your cynicism, and negativity, and keep fighting! Release the tightness across your chest and bask in God's love despite any late-night rants. No longer must you hold your breath, hoping your foibles will not be revealed.

These are the stories of your life. How you tell them matters. It takes spiritual backbone to not blame and criticize. Taking responsibility for your part helps you boldly move toward soul health. Inhale the relief such exposure offers as you release the humiliation or stress caused by it. Though it might feel scary to face true thoughts in your heart, pray now for courage:

O God, Lord of my soul, peel back my layers of criticalness, blame-shifting, and hypocrisy. Show me the anger and bitterness lurking in the shadows. I long to rise above all of this. God, please clear the way so a new path forward will open up. I understand my soul will only be as strong as I am honest about what is happening inside of me. Thank you for guiding me, for your mercy and gentleness with my heart. Amen.

Breathing Deeper

1. As you embrace better soul strength you will need large doses of self-forgiveness, kindness, and patience. What does this look like?
2. What circumstances in your life might keep you awake at night? How can you address it to get some relief?
3. God never wastes a drop of tears or an ounce of your pain. What is your response to this thought?

PART FOUR

Transformed Soul

HAVING AN UNBLEMISHED SOUL isn't feasible. No one gets through life without soul wounds. And when we do seek recovery and transformation for our wounds, it's not like our injuries are magically erased as if they never occurred. Getting over emotional injuries can prove elusive because soul transformation is difficult. It takes a brave person (you!) to move past an injury. If healing were easy, if letting go of pain and difficulty was effortless, no one would be walking around feeling stuck and unsure how to move past it. Reclaiming health in our soul requires effort to grow and improve. Turning to God with your wounds is how you bring forth your beautiful soul.

As we have been discussing, take the first step by adopting a new perspective on the injury. Keep your eyes fixed on God's desire to connect with you and transform your soul. Let this thought keep you grounded as you move toward healing.

A Gentle Journey

In the last section, we dealt with the murky waters of woundedness that can seep through your soul. I pray you have felt your conviction grow as you have discovered areas needing restoration. I pray, too, that you have been tender with yourself and others in the process.

Gentleness toward yourself is imperative. When you nurture your soul with kindness, you are calmer, more peaceful, and better equipped to take on whatever challenges come your way. Author Chris Germiel teaches, "A moment of self-compassion . . . can change your entire day. A string of such moments can change the course of your life."[10] The idea of stringing several positive thoughts together lifts my spirit and builds my confidence.

I have felt inadequate while writing this book because sometimes my soul feels "too far gone!" I ask myself whether my failings disqualify me from expressing my experiences. It feels easier to be self-critical and uncertain rather than compassionate and gentle with myself in my own journey. It has taken more than a few conversations with other wounded healers to galvanize me to press on.

One evening I shared my tussle to finish a portion of the book with my cousin, a long-time missionary to Nepal and India. It struck a chord as he said, "You are doing important work in your writing and remember who *doesn't* want you to write it."

Well, that made me sit up and listen!

He reminded me that my work matters and that there is an enemy working against my efforts. Craig's words made me want to fight back against the forces trying to stop me. Every day there is a spiritual battle between light and darkness, good and evil. It is a battle we must win!

The choice is ours to resist the dark schemes that fight against a soul that is whole.

The Truth About Recovery

Don't be fooled by false ideas of what it means to heal the wounds in your soul. Don't imagine that you must have everything settled in your heart, corrected and in place, before you can approach God. There is no linear route to soul health. It is more like up and around, down and back, over and under and up again with each step taking you to a deeper understanding of who you are and what your heart's desire truly is. Don't be surprised if you stumble along as you are learning the principles of solid soul care.

The objective is not a perfect soul, but a beautiful soul.

To achieve such a goal means resisting the darkness that can smother the flame in your heart; it means filling your mind with light and love.

Consider what transformation *is not*:

It *is not* achieving some level of perfection.

It *is not* the absence of difficult days.

It *is not* reaching a certain point of soul health where you no longer need to reflect on your soul's condition.

It *is not* a magical force field that keeps you from difficulties if you obey all the rules.

It *is not* a clenched-teeth determination to be whole.

It *is not* a solitary journey.

What spiritual transformation *is*:

It *is* an ongoing quest to discover more about God's love.

It *is* holding onto hope and breathing in God's mercy even when you trip and fall.

It *is* staying on the right path regardless of what others do or say.

It *is* getting up and trying again (and again).

It *is* leaning into the sacred ground of self-reflection.

It *is* changing perspectives.

It *is* allowing others to know you deeply as you bring soul issues into the light.

Don't fear your brokenness. Don't circle around the life you long for and wish yours was better. Instead, face your wounds head-on, be intentional about recovery, and live in alignment with the soul you really want. Along the way, accept your current state, because you know God understands even your ragged places. God gets you, even though it isn't clear how he could. He meets you where you are, even in your most difficult or desperate moments. Can you see him in the midst of it? Do you hear those vibrant notes of mercy flowing through your mind as you are reminded of his presence?

He is near. He will transform you if you allow it.

When you pray to God, you release earnest thoughts from your heart and mind, not knowing exactly how those thoughts are delivered, not knowing how God hears or how he'll answer, and yet you still pray, believing that he does hear, and he will answer.

Soul restoration is the same. God asks you to let *him* restore your soul, his lovely creation, as you live out your best version of how he made you and what he has allowed in your life. As you open yourself to him, he will hear, and he will answer.

Take comfort in the truth that God knows where you are and exactly what you need. His goal now and always is the health and restoration of your soul. As you take steps to transform, God does his part to help you heal. Pray for eyes to see how he is working in your heart. Trust him with your life.

As Earnest Hemmingway wrote,

We are all broken. That's how the light gets in.

12

Known by God

"If we want the rewards of being loved, we have to submit to the mortifying ordeal of being known."
—Tim Kreider

AT A NATIONAL CHAIN PHARMACY where I occasionally get prescriptions filled, I asked a question about a vaccine. The pharmacist asked for my name. When I gave it she replied, "Oh yeah, sure, Janet Marks" Why this made my heart swell I cannot say, but I was surprised to be known by name. It made me feel important to be recognized in a place I generally feel small among hundreds of patrons.

How much more astonishing is the fact that I am known by the God of the universe! Picture God saying, "Oh sure, it's [Insert your name here]."

Not only is he *that* familiar with your name, but he is also intimately familiar with everything in your soul. To God, you are not a number or a symbol or just one more person in a long line of people. He sees you. But sometimes we struggle to grasp God's view of us.

It's no wonder we grapple because we tend to see ourselves based on our actions—particularly the actions we are not proud of. We imagine that God is disappointed in us, that we don't measure up, or that he is angry at mistakes we have made. We know all too well that we are often quick to complain, criticize, and judge others, and feel impatient when life is hard. We might say to ourselves, "I feel aggravated with myself. Why wouldn't God feel the same?"

But here is where the road divides. We see only from one small life while God sees from quite a different vantage point. His love is unconditional, his sight is unending, and his pursuit of you never ceases.

From Scripture we understand that God formed us and knows every single thing that has transpired in our life. Consider this thought, "As a father has compassion on his children, so the Lord has compassion on those who fear him; for he knows how we are formed, he remembers we are dust" (Psalm 103:13-14).

What?!

I got a brilliant flash of hope the first time I comprehended the meaning of this scripture and wept with relief as I read it.

He remembers I am dust. Dust!

Just knowing that God grasps my frailty—knowing that I am so deeply understood by my Creator—thrilled me! God gets that we are frail.

How wonderful to serve a God who formed me, knows how I was made, and loves me. So, yes, God knows it all, and he loves me still.

Unfailing Love

The prophet Isaiah describes the expanse between us like this, "For my thoughts are not your thoughts, neither are your ways my ways, declares the LORD. As the heavens are higher than the earth, so are my ways higher than yours and my thoughts than your thoughts" (Isaiah 55:8-9).

God sees me differently than I see myself.

On dark days when you battle with wounds in your soul and search for a flicker of goodness within, being known by the God of the universe should help you feel there could be hope for "even me." It offers a handhold to grab onto, and you can seize it for support and strength to stand.

You are known by God—in spite of any faltering faith—yet still loved with a perfect love.

Our love, however, is imperfect, and we tend to expect God will love us in the same way. We sometimes assume he loves us conditionally, as people might do. Even those who claim to love us can be judgmental and condemning at times, or even withdraw or abandon us. It isn't all that surprising that we presume God will act the same. We might also assume that God's love is reserved for those who are more deserving, for those who don't appear to stumble or falter.

Though it may be tempting to think this way, please understand these are false assumptions; remember, we don't see the way God does.

God's love is faultless and unfailing and completely unchained! The God who created your soul loves you *no matter what*. And when this love dawns on you, it leaves you breathless. Allow his goodness to bring you hope. Let it increase your faith and your readiness to be seen more deeply.

Unerring Sight

King David must have felt incredibly secure in God's love as he prayed, "God, investigate my life; get all the facts firsthand. I'm an open book to you; even from a distance, you know what I'm thinking . . . I'm never out of your sight. You know everything I'm going to say before I start the first sentence" (Psalm 139:1-6, MSG).

How remarkable to understand that God can see it all—and yet ask outright for a deeper investigation. Such extreme openness is a sign of someone who believes that God will gently and caringly accomplish the needed soul work.

Sometimes we hesitate to ask God to show us the depths because we worry how he will answer. Like on the days I am afraid to pray for a trusting heart because I fret about what his answer might be. (Are you familiar with the scenario where you pray for patience and on that very day everyone moves like a snail, gets in your way, and pushes all your buttons? Sure, it's an opportunity to grow your patience, but tell me, who naturally wants patience that badly?) So my faulty reasoning goes like this: If I simply don't ask for growth of a particular quality, perhaps I won't be challenged to change.

It is laughable to think reverse psychology will work on God. Remember who we are dealing with! Doesn't he know every single thought and motive of the heart, even those we try to keep under wraps?

Although your inclination may lean heavily toward resisting growth or hiding your brokenness, down deep in your heart you are keenly aware he already knows it all. Being open to God "seeing and showing" you things in your life is vital for your soul's transformation.

Unlimited Thoughts

Not only does God know you and see you, but he thinks beautiful thoughts about you. Another prayer of David boggles the mind, "How precious also are your thoughts for me, God! How vast is the sum of them! Were I to count them, they would outnumber the grains of sand" (Psalm 139:17-18).

Precious thoughts!

This is what God thinks about not only David but about you. He doesn't think just one or two precious thoughts about you but more thoughts than there are grains of sand!

Try to grasp the immensity of such devotion. You are on God's mind. Invite him in, and he will kindly and gently help you to heal the areas that are holding you back.

There are many reasons you may want to run away from God or try to hide. Maybe you have attempted to transform your soul over and over but failed or you've become weary of doing the right thing and don't want to keep trying. It can be tempting to turn and walk away. Maybe your heart is plagued with doubt or disillusionment, and you decide to seek elsewhere for answers. Whatever your reason, even on the days you don't understand what God is trying to do in your life, remember, he still sees you and thinks of you.

Being loved, being seen, and being thought of doesn't equal a life free from tough times. Sometimes we want to believe God will coat us with a protective layer of Teflon if we follow him. If we hold to the rules, then we won't experience disappointment or have our soul pierced.

When we face struggles, it often surprises us. But the truth is that faith is not some talisman given to protect our souls from harm. Nowhere does God promise that our souls will never be injured in this life. And the reality is that during our time on earth, our wounded souls may never be *completely* healed and restored.

The apostle James challenges our view of hardships: "When all kinds of trials and temptations crowd into your lives, don't resent them as intruders, but welcome them as friends!" (James 1:2, PHILLIPS)

Seriously? As friends? Welcoming tough times with wide open arms is generally not my go-to response. But as I read the next verse, I realize that these challenging times "come to test your faith and to produce in you the quality of endurance" (James 1:3, PHILLIPS). This reminds me that the difficulty of achieving soul health is the very thing that allows me to transform.

Even challenging days have some good in them! Find the good and allow it to flood your lungs with light as you breathe this prayer:

Lord, God, fill me with your light when I can't find my way. I know you are aware of my true reaction to tough days. Help me to do better and learn to welcome them as I would my friends. You think precious thoughts about me even though I barely understand your might. No matter the struggles I face, no matter the disappointments or hurts I endure, you see me and you haven't forgotten me. What a comfort to me that you know my name. Amen

Breathing Deeper

1. To God, you are not a number or a symbol or just one more person in a long line of people. In what ways does this thought refresh your soul?
2. Write down some precious thoughts God has about you.
3. What is one way a challenging time has transformed your soul? How have you welcomed it "as a friend"?

13

Uniquely You

"God has given you a fingerprint that no one else has to leave an imprint no one else can."
—Keith Craft

I AM A PEOPLE-WATCHER. WHILE waiting for a flight at the Denver International Airport, hundreds of people walked by, all shapes and sizes. The thought occurred to me that in addition to their obvious outward differences each one most certainly had a distinctive personality. Not only that, but they each had unique innate abilities and individual upbringings. As I considered these ideas, it astounded me to realize they have also all had different influences, educations, and life experiences. Everyone was incredibly unique.

Since this is so, why is anyone surprised that each person may experience a unique connection with God?

When you look at your fingers under the light do you wonder why God created you with those exact fingerprints? Amazingly, there is a one in 64 *trillion* (that's 64 followed by twelve zeros) chance someone could have your identical print. Even identical twins' prints are distinctly different. This is a magnificent testimony to God's attention to detail. Did he do this to help us grasp our uniqueness and see the importance he places on each one of us?

Distinct Soul

Might your individual walk with God be as remarkably rare as your fingerprints? Could your soul's relationship with God be as unique as your fingerprint, like a customized connection with him?

Imagine. You have a signature walk with God!

Since God has created each of us individually and uniquely, this begs the question: could our individual understanding of God be similarly distinctive? It should not surprise us that he reaches out to connect with our souls using various means, whether through people, situations, experiences, circumstances, or even our individual personalities.

Since you are vastly different from the person next to you, God takes that into consideration and designs interactions that are specifically for you. Each of us loves God in our own unique way, and we draw close to him by different means.

Here is the mystery of how God restores your soul: he meets you right where you are and gives you exactly what you need.

Grasping the Divine

There is so much in this world beyond our capacity to understand; how can we think we know everything there is to know about God? Our minds can barely conceive the distance from here to the moon, let alone the inner workings of all creation. Grasping the divine is daunting.

A staggering thought comes to us from an Old Testament passage where God's servant Job describes God as the one "who suspends the earth over nothing" (Job 26:7). It takes a lot of work to wrap our finite brains around this concept. (You've got to wonder how Job knew that way back then.)

In his heady commentary, Matthew Henry writes about this passage, "The vast terraqueous globe neither rests upon any pillars nor hangs upon any axle . . . it is firmly fixed in its place, poised with its own weight. The art of man could not *hang a feather upon nothing*, yet divine wisdom hangs the whole earth so."[11]

When I read this, I laughed out loud at the irrationality of hanging a feather on nothing! (Then I went and looked up the meaning of *terraqueous*.)

Reading further in the same passage from Job, the writer reminds us that whatever our most audacious thought about God might be, anything we can possibly imagine is "but the *outer fringe* of his works; how faint the whisper we hear of him! Who then can understand the thunder of his power?" (Job 26:14, italics mine).

Can you bring your most magnificent idea about God to mind? Then imagine this is just the outer fringe of who he is and what he can do! It leaves us scratching our heads trying to grasp this concept of immeasurable proportions.

Buckle up: *This* is the God of the universe who knows *you*. *This* is the one who wants to connect with *your* soul. Closeness to God. Isn't this precisely what you are searching for? "Move your heart closer to God and he will come even closer to you." (James 4:8, TPT).

A healthy soul is a soul close to God.

Personal Connection

I imagine, if pressed, most of us believe *our* idea of walking closely with God is the only right way. And yet, could it possibly be true that *only my* concept of connecting with God is valid? Do we truly know what each person's encounter with God should look like? Can you make way for God to encounter someone in a way that differs from yours?

Sometimes it makes us uncomfortable how others connect with God or how they interpret his hand in their life. Some get nervous when others speak of some celestial event and immediately dismiss them as kooks. Others worry some charlatan will try to influence people away from God's truth.

If God is always at work to reach and help restore *every* soul, what if he meets them in a way that is unfamiliar to you? Do you believe that, in his infinite wisdom, he knows which experiences will draw them to him?

Growing up in a fundamental Christian church tradition taught me that spirituality looked only one way. I spent years believing there was only one way to correctly approach God, (*my* way). I cringe when I think about my harshness as I judged those who didn't think or act the same way as I did.

Such arrogance never reflects the heart of Jesus, regardless of how well-meaning we are.

I heard a podcaster share an exhilarating experience he had during surgery. He spoke of seeing a beautiful light surrounding the room as the surgeon worked, and he sensed God was present to assure his safety. He believed it was a personal encounter with God, and it filled him with calmness. If this is what turned his heart to God, is it up to you or me to challenge the story?

I have a friend whose beloved mother recently passed away. She said a red cardinal showed up at her kitchen window each morning for a few weeks. My friend likes to think her mom was stopping by to check on her. What a tender sentiment, to see a small creature and feel comfort. Regardless of your belief about this bird being some supernatural messenger, it gets my friend's attention, comforts her, and leads her to pray.

One woman believes that God only connects with her through the pages of her Bible. She is skeptical of any outside influence that counters her understanding of Scripture. If this is what works for her, is it our job to judge her attempt to connect with God? He is more than able to work through her principles and find a way to reveal himself to her.

Connection with God plays a vital part in soul recovery, and he will do whatever is needed to get your attention. I can't say that someone's experience of hearing thunder that shook the ground like elephants stomping past was not from God. I can't say what occurs for everyone is or is not from God, but I do know he wants a relationship with *every* person.

How does God speak to *you*?

Let the joy of being uniquely created and personally connected with God touch your heart as you pray these words:

> *God, you astound me with your desire to be close to me. Hover over my soul. Help me be gracious as you are gracious, to show kindness to those who connect with you differently than I do. That you suspend this earth over nothing reminds me of your power. My mind can barely conceive the outer fringe of who you are. That you make an effort to reach and restore my soul, I can only utter my humble gratitude. Amen*

Breathing Deeper

1. What is your most magnificent idea about God? What does this mean for your own soul health?
2. Do you believe God is striving to reach and restore every soul? Can you see how he may reach them differently than he does you? How will this be evidenced in your life?
3. Since you are vastly different from the person next to you, how might God tailor your individual interactions with him?

14

Soul Bound

"We are each of us angels with only one wing, and we can only fly embracing each other."
—Luciano de Crescenzo

IT TAKES COURAGE TO BARE your soul.

The quote by de Crescenzo asserts that to fly efficiently as one-winged angels, we must lean on another person and share their wing to fly straight. You lean on someone, they lean back.

With whom do you share a wing? Who traverses life's journey with you? These are the sojourners that help you see more objectively, support you when you're discouraged, and spur you on to try again.

If a name comes to your mind, it indicates that you have bravely shared your fears, storms, and inadequacies with someone whom you trust. If you can't think of anyone, you may need to take more initiative to experience being soul bound. Take small steps forward and start to build such a relationship so you have someone on whom to lean.

In her book *Gifts of Imperfection* Brené Brown speaks articulately about vulnerability. She writes about being real and vulnerable and has a mantra she tells herself: "Don't shrink. Don't puff up. Stand on your sacred ground."[12]

Avoid these two extremes as you share your soul journey:

- Don't shrink back and hide in shame.
- Don't be prideful and unwilling to learn from others.

Instead, find a humble balance. Don't give up when you swing too far to either side. Keep trying to find the right balance. It takes practice.

We may think we can't be vulnerable because no one else struggles the way we do. When my head gets jumbled due to some perplexing circumstance, if I ignore it, my fears and the issues grow big and unwieldy. When I confide in a friend, much of the murkiness disappears because speaking it out loud shines light into the shadows and offers some objectivity. Talking it through helps produce possible solutions.

Never Alone

While speaking at a virtual conference on the topic of forgiveness, I asked the approximately two hundred listeners about areas of their life in which they needed to experience forgiveness. The chat box came alive as many shared,

"I need forgiveness for my pride."

"I need help with my grumpiness."

"I'm told I'm a poor listener."

"I am too judgmental."

"I need to learn about grace since I seem to assume the worst."

"I complain too much."

"I act too self-righteous."

"I am afraid of getting close and am told I act 'distant' and avoid people."

"Told I'm too snippy."

"I need forgiveness for jumping to conclusions."

I shouldn't have been surprised how easily the listeners knew exactly where they needed mercy, because we all have such areas in our lives. But their willingness to put it out there into cyberspace was remarkable, and humbling. The exercise reminds me that as different as we are from one another, we all have the same needs. We often remain isolated and afraid to share our lives with others. We think we are an exception and can manage this soul journey alone. This is simply not true. No one does soul recovery alone.

The perspective you get from other people is invaluable. Their objectivity helps clear out fuzzy and faulty reasoning, such as:

- I am worse than others.
- I should be further along by now.
- My faith is substandard.
- I've tried to live for God, but it feels hopeless.
- My failures cannot be rectified.
- I am a disappointment to God.
- I am unlovable due to my sin.
- No one can relate to me or understand me.
- I don't matter.
- I feel embarrassed about my actions (lies, bad habits, regretful words).

Pretending all is okay in your soul can lead to bone-crushing weariness. If you are trying to hold up a false front to appear better or different than you truly are, the people who love you love only your façade. The relationship will always remain shallow because you don't let it go deep. Is love *really* love if it is based on a façade? A good friend is someone who knows you well. They will know something is up behind that mask and say something about it.

Revealing the inner workings of your heart takes a big dose of courage, but those with whom your soul is bound will help you focus on steady and more sensible thoughts. They will remind you that everyone struggles with their faith, that you are not alone, and that God's love is bigger and wider than you can fathom.

There is something powerful about sharing your stories—the good stories as well as the unpleasant ones. You need people who know you and will speak truth to you, offer support, laugh with you, cry with you, or simply sit with you in silence when that is all you can manage.

At lunch one day, I asked two friends for input about a conversation I planned to have with an adult child who was making some concerning choices. I was feeling agitated about it, so there was no surprise when I came across as irritated and judgmental.

With raised eyebrows, both friends asked me some clarifying questions: "What do you hope the conversation will accomplish?" "Is it your intention to shame your child into acting the way you want?" "Do you believe such an approach will be well received?"

I swallowed. Hard.

Neither of them joined in on my tirade. No, these soul-bound friends offered much-needed wisdom and gently challenged my faulty thinking by stating, "Maybe, rather than attacking or criticizing, you might ask more questions and try to understand the reasons for their choices."

My puffed up reasoning deflated like a cheap air-mattress. Whoosh! Thanks to these beloved friends who know me well, I could acknowledge the impatient, critical condition of my heart.

I inhaled deeply, thinking how grateful I am to have soul-bound truth-speakers who with love and kindness nudge me to better life choices. Together they offered me a wing to help me fly straight.

Life in the Light

Jesus told those seeking to follow him, "Light has come into the world and people loved the darkness rather than the light, because their deeds were evil . . . But the one who practices the truth comes to the light" (John 3:19, 21, NET). It's up to each of us to pull aside the blackout curtains and let the light flood in.

It is so important to grapple with those dark webby shadows and not remain in the inky darkness of seclusion. Hiding gives us a false sense of safety, but it is in the dimness that we are also joined by isolation, loneliness, and fear. When we have been hurt or a trust has been broken hiding may be essential at first to get our bearings, but it is not a place in which to remain. Work to get whatever help you need, because if you stay secluded, you will miss out on amazing connections that could greatly benefit your soul.

Don't miss out!

Courage and honesty are partners in this beautiful dance of vulnerability. The Latin phrase *veritas non quaerit angulos* means "truth seeks no corners for concealment." When you are ready to share your truth, you no longer look for places to hide. You resist the urge to push the hard conversations away. You are ready to say, "Do you have a minute? I'd like to share something with you." This was the approach I needed to embrace with my adult child. Certainly, an honest talk was warranted but within the parameters of love and humility and a readiness to hear the other side.

On the topic of vulnerability and connection, Brené Brown shares, "When we are looking for compassion, we need someone who is deeply rooted, able to bend, and most of all, we need someone who embraces us for our strengths and struggles."[13]

So true! We long for people who will accept us for who we are and bear with us when we get stuck. To foster such a relationship requires openness and trust. We long for people who know our strengths and struggles and who don't pound on us when our thinking is faulty. Those who understand us well and know what makes us tick will speak the truth, patiently and kindly, when we need to hear it. Without the component of honesty our relationships will remain superficial.

Be patient. Learning to live like this takes time. But the benefit of attaining a beautiful soul is well worth it. In addition, you will find rich joy in being that kind of friend to someone else. Your unique gifts can help you build others up and support *their* soul journey as well. As you care for each other's souls, God will knit your hearts together.

If you believe you have little to give to help others, think again. A lovely poem often attributed to F. Scott Fitzgerald emphasizes that my "gift" doesn't have to be big; it need only be heartfelt:

> "It was only a sunny smile
> And little it cost in the giving,
> But it scattered the night.
> Like morning light,
> And made the day worth living."

A sunny smile! What a small but precious thing capable of "scattering" the night of another person! Who has God placed in your life who makes your life worth living?

Watch for ways to return the blessing.

Find Your People

Meaningful relationships are achievable.

Connections with others will deepen as you share your life freely with trusted individuals. They aren't here to "fix" you. Fixing you is not their job, but look to them for support and camaraderie. Being soul bound is about *connection*. Don't wait for others to do the work of opening their life to you. You could share one small heart concern and ask them to pray for you. Start with a light approach, and say, "I'm concerned about this area in my life" or "I'd like your input on . . ." Depth doesn't happen all at once but little by little. If you share something personal and the listener doesn't seem ready to reciprocate, be patient, but also branch out to others until you find someone in a similar frame of mind.

As your soul health improves, you will exude more peace and gratitude, which in turn will attract people who are also interested in soul care. When you open yourself up, you will draw people in who are also looking for meaningful connection. They may not even know what it is about you that draws them, but they want to be in your presence. As connections deepen, you'll find your soul being fed, refreshed, and bolstered. These are *your people*.

Thank God for the people he will send into your life as you pray:

> *Dear Lord, you know exactly with whom I need to be soul bound. Please lead us together. Something happens in my heart when I am known, a sense of safety wells up, and so I thank you for those who know me. I thank you for those who love me enough to shine your light into my shadows and share their wing with me. Give me the heart to do the same for them. Amen.*

Breathing Deeper

1. With whom are you soul bound? What does this mean to you?
2. Which conversation are you avoiding? Can you say the words, "Do you have a minute? I'd like to share something with you."
3. What is a heartfelt "gift" you can give to those in your life?

15

This Side of Heaven

"The question is not what you look at, but what you see."
—Henry David Thoreau

YOUR DECISION TO DO SOUL work is nothing less than an awakening.

Every time you choose courage over fear, honesty over hiding, and truth over a façade, you take one step further on the road to recovery, one step further on the path to a beautiful soul. Your whole life you make these right choices and find yourself beautifying your soul.

Resoluteness of the Soul

What strengthens your mind and your heart? How do you fortify your convictions? Consider this quote by author Mark Manson and think deeply about what motivates you to make better choices. "Bravery is not the absence of fear. Bravery is feeling the fear, the doubt, the insecurity, and deciding something else is more important."[14]

What is significant enough that pushes you to overcome discomfort or distress as you strive for spiritual recovery?

What is that *something else* that is more important to you?" Why do you want soul health? What motivates you to develop a bold and beautiful soul? The importance you give to soul health will be evident by how you live. Consider these three examples of people who figured out their *something else* and changed how they lived as a result:

>A therapist asked a client struggling with loneliness: "What is the *worst* thing that could happen if you let others in and shared your heart?" The client answered, "If they really knew me, they might reject me; then I'd be alone." The therapist calmly responded, "You have told me you feel lonely now. If you won't open your life to others, you're already living your worst nightmare."
>
>What was more important to this client: Her fear of being *known* or her desire to not be lonely? She decided to open her heart and let a few trusted friends know what was going on inside. Her life was changed because of this choice.

>Another man told me about the rocky relationship he had with his father, and yet in our conversation I was surprised how pleasantly he spoke about his dad. When I asked about it, the man said, "I decided to get past my resentment, and we finally made a good connection before he died. I'm grateful I lived long enough to outlive my bitterness." That comment stopped me in my tracks!
>
>By having the boldness to make a decision, the man gained these remarkable gifts:
>
>>Time to heal and gain fresh perspective.
>>Time to forgive one who had caused injury.
>>A connection that had not been there before.
>>No regrets.

Which was more important to this man: standing his bitter ground or reconciling a difficult relationship and being able to remember his dad without pain?

A friend of mine is earnestly working to overcome arrogance and stop looking with disdain toward those who don't act like him, believe like him, and think like him. He admits it when he fails and prays to be more gracious and Christlike. For him, it's more important to overcome his arrogance than to remain in it. What a gift!

All of these people made a decision. They could cling to the rot of an unhealthy soul or begin making better choices. No doubt hard days were involved, but the peace of mind they enjoyed by making the better choice far outweighs their discomfort. Their better life choices lead them to greater soul health.

Ask yourself these questions:

- Are truth and openness more valuable to you than hiding or pretending?
- Is forgiveness more important than bitterness?
- Is reconciliation in a relationship more satisfying than hanging on to an old grudge?
- Is freedom more important to you than the temporary rush or moment of comfort from continuing to practice a bad habit?
- Is there someone you love to whom you want to be a better example of making healthy choices?

Henry David Thoreau cautioned, "We must learn to reawaken and keep ourselves awake, not by mechanical aids, but by an infinite expectation of the dawn." As you build your soul health, keep your eyes on the dawn, the hope of a new day.

Don't stop working at spiritual growth. You will need staying power to work through tender spots and make the hard decisions to course correct.

To truly enjoy a health-filled soul means you work at it your whole life.

Backbone of the Soul

An old friend frequently says, "The best of us is a mess." Although this truth is hard to admit, we can agree it takes a strong backbone to say, "I am messy, I make mistakes" out loud. It can be jarring to take a close look and realize the weaknesses in your soul. You may stumble along as you learn how to process what you've discovered, but take heart, each new insight builds your stamina and helps transform you.

Whatever tensions or stresses you feel about your flaws, there is also new stability and steadiness coming right alongside them. As you give close attention to the matters in your soul, strength will naturally follow, just as a well-aimed arrow will fly toward its goal.

When we step back and reassess where we are and where we want to be, we can find ourselves making surprising progress.

In *The Book of Common Courage*, author K. J. Ramsey sums up how we make progress in our life. "Blessed are you who push through dirt year after year, day after day, choosing kindness over criticism, forgiveness over fury, and trust in the truth that beauty will eventually bloom."[15]

Your daily decisions to press through will yield stunning results. Pray now and ask God for the conviction to continue your soul work every day, this side of eternity.

O God, I need your staying power to push through my dirt and work through the tender places of my heart. When I struggle to face difficult things, please quiet my fears and strengthen my hands for the task. As long as I am on this side of heaven, grant me bravery and willingness to release all that keeps me from the vital soul work. Amen.

Breathing Deeper

1. Why does it work best for you to do just a little soul work each day? How does this impact your whole life?
2. Every time you choose to be honest about your inner self, it's one step further on the path to a beautiful soul. What one step can you take today?
3. "Bravery is feeling the fear, the doubt, the insecurity and deciding something else is more important." What is the *something else* for you?

16

Which Path?

"Like a plant that starts up in showers and sunshine and does not know which has best helped it to grow, it is difficult to say whether the hard things or the pleasant things did the most good."
—Lucy Larcom

WHEN YOU REALIZE THE PATH you are on isn't transforming your soul's health, it's time to change routes.

At a luncheon I was seated next to a fellow named Andreas. During our conversation, we talked about how hard it is for people to change thought patterns. Andreas shared about a counseling session during which his therapist suggested he rethink his approach to a particular issue by visualizing himself walking through a field. The counselor said if he walked on the same path day after day, the ground under his feet would become solid and easy to navigate, and he would naturally follow it to the same place. But if Andreas wanted to end up in a different location with a different outcome, he must choose a new path, even though it felt unfamiliar or even awkward at times.

His story reminded me of traveling on the expansive underground subway system while my family lived in Germany as missionaries. Several times I took the wrong train and ended up far from home. As soon as I realized I wasn't where I wanted to be, staying on the wrong train, no matter how comfortable I was in my seat, would be counterproductive. To get home, I had to disembark, buy another ticket, and board a train traveling in the other direction.

If you hang on to your long-rehearsed negative thoughts, how will you grow spiritually stronger? If you remain unwilling to forgive someone who hurt you, how will you achieve a grace-filled life? And if you continue down the familiar path of hiding your true self, how will you ever build meaningful connections?

Instead of slogging along your predictable, typical, standard route, why not intentionally create a new thought path or make the choice to go in a different direction? Don't allow your present day to be governed by your yesterday. Some of the following ideas might help you get started:

- *Spend time* with those whose path you admire and learn from them: initiate, ask questions, observe, and imitate. Even if it's a long distance, pick up the phone and invite input. I was once asked to mentor a friend halfway around the world. She wanted feedback on her life, parenting, marriage, and ministry. Distance didn't stop her desire to grow.
- *Be honest* about the actual condition of your soul. Humbly acknowledge your needs and allow others to help you on your journey.
- *Read a book* by a new-to-you or different type of author. Branch out. You may not agree with every point in the book, but you will undoubtedly come away with new insights and wisdom.
- *Read your Bible in another translation.* It can be uplifting to hear familiar concepts with a fresh mindset.
- *Visualize* a negative memory deflating and fading away.

Navigating a new path can feel uncomfortable. Sticking with what's familiar appears simpler, and may *be* simpler, but you will arrive right back at the same place every time. When change is called for, finding an unfamiliar path to a new destination requires effort, perseverance, and intent.

Walk This Way

God never leaves you without a guide. And though he gives you the ability to consider and choose the direction of your feet, he will show you the best path if you let him.

In the time of Isaiah and the prophets, God promised to guide his followers in the way they should go. "Your ears will hear sweet words behind you: 'Go this way. There is your path; this is how you should go' whenever you must decide whether to turn to the right or the left" (Isaiah 30:21 VOICE).

The thought of "sweet words behind you" feels reassuring, as if someone is watching out for you, whispering words of encouragement and instruction. And indeed, God is here, helping you find the way.

A longtime friend, Robin, often refers to the passage above when making a significant decision. The verse offers what she calls her Guide of Three:

1. Go this way.
2. There is your path.
3. This is how you should go.

Seeking her best way forward, she aims to please God with her life, prays earnestly for clarity, and then keeps watch for nudges from God. If she finds three affirmative signs, it helps her make her decision.

The push from God might arise as she reads Scripture or engages in a random conversation. It may come as an open door of opportunity or as she seeks input from those who know her well.

It's an interesting practice that has been a help to her.

For years, Robin felt disappointment about not completing her college degree. She prayed about going back to school but was unsure about the timing and the cost. One day she had a chance meeting with a neighbor on a morning walk, which led to a series of conversations that led to her being offered a job at a nearby university.

When she learned that university employees received free tuition, she sensed God was offering her some direction, through (1) a chance meeting of a neighbor, (2) an unexpected job offer, and (3) the possibility of free tuition.

Coincidence? Robin says no. She believes it was God nudging her to contemplate a return to school to finish her degree.

In a letter to Timothy, the apostle Paul urges him to "Reflect on what I am saying, for the Lord will give you insight into all this" (2 Timothy 2:7). How would God provide Timothy with insight? We don't know the details, but we *do* know that Paul said the Lord would give Timothy insight, which tells us that God does work in our thoughts to give us understanding and discernment.

What form do you imagine God's *insight* in your life might take? Will it come through:

A door opening?

Wise counsel from a friend?

God's spirit placing an idea in your mind?

Since it is God's desire to restore and transform your soul, why wouldn't he open your mind to understand? What he asks of you is to love and obey him, to open your ears, eyes, and heart to hear his gentle instruction.

Oswald Chambers, known for his outstanding book *My Utmost for His Highest* wrote: "Obey God in the thing he shows you and instantly the next thing is opened. God will never reveal more truth about himself until you have obeyed what you know already."[16]

Part of being on the right track with God is obedience to what you already know. It is *never* from God if you hear some insight that diminishes Scripture or calls you away from obedience. He speaks clearly through his word; you can always breathe in his truth, listen for insight, and obey what you know.

God will reveal himself as he chooses. As the soundness of your soul returns, you will be amazed at the truths you never knew about yourself and your God.

Curves Ahead

Some days you may feel that God is distant and hard to reach, refusing to answer when you cry out for direction. You may feel abandoned or forgotten and be tempted to give in to frustration or throw up your hands and quit trying to attain a soul that is whole. But this is precisely the best time to remember what you know to be true about God: his goodness seeks you out, and he loves you no matter how many walls you've erected. God is faithful and "he will never leave you or forsake you" (Deuteronomy 31:6). His words will gently call you back from the edge of despair.

Can you trust him even when life doesn't feel clear, and trust that he has a purpose behind any soul injury or challenging situation? Laura Story wrote a profound song called "Blessings," that reminds us God's goodness may show up in a surprising way. In whatever form God breaks your heart, he holds it tenderly in his hands and will mold it into blessings beyond belief. As the song says, sometimes the trial coming at us in our life is just mercy in disguise.

What if he has used adversity to rescue you from something even more terrible? What if the difficulty is some part of an even greater deliverance? When you pray to God to be delivered from some hardship and don't immediately see the answer you want, will you trust him?

Job certainly struggled with the difficult days. His friend, Elihu reminded him that, "God delivers them through the affliction itself, and uses the trial to open their ears to His voice" (Job 36:15, VOICE).

Wow! The maker of your soul delivers you and opens your ears to hear his voice. On your most challenging days, God finds a way to expand your heart and open your mind to him.

We may not see the deliverance when we are in the middle of a storm, but when we look back on the trouble, we can clearly list the ways God showed up on our behalf and guided us lovingly to the other side. In hindsight, we can often see what we have learned about ourselves, about others, and about God.

Author, Kate Bowler, who battled back from Stage IV colon cancer, said that as God accompanied her to the very edge, her only prayer was this: "God, save me, save me, save me. And God, if you don't, love me through."[17] She learned to surrender and to trust through an awful time in her life. Of course, she hated learning the "lessons," but now she looks back and sees the broader spectrum of God's participation in her journey. She uses what she learned to guide others and help them find the blessing in their difficulties.

We can always use a dose of healthy perspective. A gray-haired woman listened as her friend despaired about the arrest of her college daughter, the night before. The police showed up at a party and hauled everyone off to jail, the daughter included. The woman listened closely, nodding as the distressed mother asked what she should do.

The older woman smiled, patted the friend on the shoulder, and said, "Be patient and love her. Right now, your daughter is just working on her testimony and one day she will use this experience to help others believe they too can learn and grow through poor life choices." What a valuable perspective on a difficult day.

Similarly, Henri Nouwen, a Theology Professor at Notre Dame and Yale, suggested we embrace this valuable principle when we experience injury. He wrote, "The first step to healing is not to step away from pain, but toward it."

Lean into the discomfort. In every facet—every affliction, every "coincidence," every person God sends your way—open your ears, listen, and let him reach your heart.

Be patient and kind to yourself and be realistic. Remember that not every issue in your soul will be completely resolved simply by leaning in. Chip away at your standard responses and adjust your behavior along the way. You still have many unfinished, imperfect parts, yet it is within your capability to deepen your closeness with God.

Soul care is a journey *for life*. Choose your path wisely and pray now:

> *O my God, my hands lie open to you today. Show me the path that will lead me to you. If in transforming my soul a change of direction is needed, strengthen my resolve to walk on the better path and remind me that you remain steady and near. On hard days, I'm tempted to erect walls between us. Help me remember you hold my brokenness tenderly in your hands. Help me find purpose in my pain. Amen.*

Breathing Deeper

1. What do you imagine God's insight to you would look or sound like?
2. Recall a way God has used a "difficulty" to open your ears. What did you learn about yourself? What did you learn about others?
3. Which difficulty in your life can you lean into?

PART FIVE

Beautiful Soul

THE BRITISH FILM *CHARIOTS OF FIRE,* released in 1981, is based on the true story of two runners training for the 1924 Olympic Games in Paris. The movie tells the story of athlete Eric Liddle, a devout Christian and the son of missionaries to China. When asked why he runs, Eric says, "God made me fast. And when I run, I feel his pleasure."[18] Let that thought resonate for a moment. Feeling God's pleasure is a remarkable standard upon which to base your life.

In which moments of your life do you feel God's pleasure? Are there times when you sense the warmth of his smile beaming in your direction? Imagine what God sees when he looks at this earth and observes so much darkness. I like to think that in that sea of shadow, my tiny, winking flame can be seen by him and brings him some kind of joy.

Do you ever wonder whether God is pleased with how you live? Is he pleased when:

- You get up each time you're knocked down?
- You serve and help others?
- You give of yourself, your talents, and your time?
- You do what is right in the face of adversity?

These traits describe someone with a beautiful soul. Such people are self-aware and genuine. They help others feel valued, they are kind, and they possess a gracious and compassionate nature. Beautiful souls convey honesty, concern, humility, and gratitude. Their unfeigned concern shines brightly and chases the shadows from every corner.

Certainly, there are many words that can be used to describe a beautiful soul. Which ones would describe your soul?

When my brother heard my plan to dedicate this book to our mom, he asked if the book was about her. I said no but then reconsidered. Yes, it is about her. I learned most of what I know about a beautiful soul from observing her life and her actions. Her impact was incandescent, filled to the brim with God's spiritual gifts. She had a bona fide love for people that captivated them and drew them in. They somehow understood she was genuinely interested in their lives. A beautiful soul indeed.

Imagine hearing someone say, "You have a beautiful soul." I doubt there is a kinder accolade to be found. Receiving such a compliment is within the realm of possibility.

A beautiful soul is attainable!

Heart of Gold

People who are honest, humble, grateful, and show genuine concern for others have what we might say a heart of gold, twenty-four carat gold! Unsurprisingly, they are the ones with whom we want to be friends and allow their kindness and openheartedness to touch us. We are drawn to such people. We long for the warmth of their sunny soul to fall on our shoulders. Such a life has an impact and attracts us to them.

Ray Charles said, "What is a soul? It's like electricity. We don't really know what it is, but it's a force that can light up a room."

Aim for a beautiful soul. Be the person who lights up the room when you walk in!

17

An Honorable Soul

"All you can change is yourself. But sometimes that changes everything."
—Gary W. Goldstein

IT WAS HIGH SUMMER, AND several longtime girlfriends and I were enjoying a day on the lake. I stood at the back of the pontoon boat, capturing video footage of Suzanne, who was flying like the wind on an inner tube as we soared across the water. Suzanne signaled the boat driver to slow down.

Renee, still getting a feel for the controls, nudged the throttle back, and it cut the power fast. The quick stop sent me tumbling topsy-turvy across the boat. I had barely righted myself when Suzanne signaled to "go." Renee gunned it, and off we roared, once more upending me across the deck in the other direction.

Finally, getting back on my feet and able to catch my breath, I exclaimed, "Renee! Pay attention!" Did she even notice I was flopping all over the boat? Of course, she hadn't. Her eyes were on the water ahead, which was precisely where they should have been!

We laughed ourselves silly as we became aware that the entire double cartwheel episode had been recorded on my camera.

But really, who needed to be paying attention?

It should have been me. Anyone knows if you are on a boat, you brace yourself, hold on, and prepare for rogue waves, turns, or fast stops. How interesting that my first reaction was to blame someone else.

It is so easy to blame others when you slip up rather than face your own weakness or harmful patterns. Succumbing to this tendency means you are shifting the blame or trying to avoid accountability. If you recognize this in yourself, be patient and kind as you untangle and comb through your tendency to pass the buck.

Taking responsibility for your mistakes is honorable; it means you can be trusted to say what is true and act, accordingly, not blame someone else. Changing this behavior happens deep inside when you intentionally choose to live this way. We are called to not "conform to the pattern of this world but be transformed by the renewing of your mind" (Romans 12:2).

Honor comes through mind renewal.

It's understandable when you are tired, disappointed, afraid, or embarrassed that you let go of your conviction to be honorable. Those "less than desirable" emotions sometimes emerge, blowing like Old Faithful. They bubble and snap under the surface as the pressure builds and then blow boiling sulfurous water high and hard.

In those moments when your deep desire to be honorable flies out the window, remember to be patient and kind to yourself, adjust your actions, and return to building an honorable mindset.

Big Soul

Aristotle, a towering figure in ancient Greek philosophy, praised the virtue of megalopsychia (mega-lo-SIK-ia). It's hard to say but not so hard to understand. Bear with me as we geek out on this fascinating thought.

Megalopsychia means "greatness of soul" and can also be translated as "magnanimity" or "big generosity." Someone who exhibits megalopsychia is openhanded, considerate, and decent. Such a person is generous in spirit, and they display greatness of mind and dignity of soul.

When we look at the Latin for this word, we get *magas* ("big" or "great") and *psūkhé* ("soul" or "spirit"). Wait for it . . . "big soul"!

Wow! Who doesn't want some of this?

Grasping the deeper meaning behind these words sent a shiver through me as the richness of living with such qualities became clear. The world can use more big soul!

To have a big or honorable soul means you are considerate and gracious, while humbly trusting the hand God has dealt to you. How do you get this big soul?

Small Steps to a Big Soul

Your personal uprightness is built choice by choice and day by day. It is the little steps taken in the best direction that create your big soul. Yet, who has time for self-reflection every day, let alone has the *ummph* to do it? Seriously, when was the last time you did anything day after day, let alone dig around in the well-guarded depths of your heart?

Any time you hesitate to look deeper, you lose out on the potential for personal growth. Though it might seem scary, doing the *daily* work to achieve this big, honorable soul will bring meaning and self confidence to your days. You will need to resist your fears of being exposed and combat the weaknesses that trip you up.

Jesus reminds us, "Be careful how you listen, for whoever has [a teachable heart], to him more [understanding] will be given" (Luke 8:18, AMP). What are you being taught or shown as you consider your soul's condition? The more pliable and teachable your heart is, the more your understanding will deepen.

Becoming self-aware can feel sharply uncomfortable. Even so, it is a huge part of developing honor. It is helpful to look toward the motivation behind your actions. No more hiding or pretending. Instead, you are honest about what you find and humbly ask for help. Self-awareness is giving honest attention to whatever is brewing inside.

To grow and maintain an honorable soul asks you to find:

- Courage to move away from the damaging habits of concealment.
- Tenacity to shine a light into those pesky problem areas lurking around corners.
- Honesty to allow others to know you.
- Humility to let others help you.

This means you will be making some changes. (Hard swallow.)

Yes, change usually feels scary.

Here is the good news: You only need to make *one* small change at a time. All must not be conquered in a day! Just figure out one small area you can approach and begin there. Decide you want to change it and then make a realistic plan. Put one thing into action. When (not if) you falter, get up and try again.

Once you decide you want an honorable soul, God sends you what you need to achieve it. This assignment came into my inbox via a weekly newsletter:

Sometime today look at yourself in the mirror. Don't cringe or criticize. Instead, say a simple thank you. Because, truly, you are a beautiful creation, fashioned in love by God. Then ask God to create *irresistible beauty* inside, where it counts. In this moment, right now, you have a beautiful soul. Rest and rejoice in that.

If I'm being completely honest, I can admit there had been no small amount of cringing, self-criticizing, and struggling in my heart while writing about developing a beautiful soul. But since it is God who is helping me to build honor, why would I be so surprised that this email happened to show up right when it did? The newsletter offered such a tender gift, a needed reminder that God placed this incredible soul in me, his prized possession!

Let his kindness soothe your soul as you meet with him right here, right now and create honor in your life. Rest in this place and be reminded how precious and loved you are as you pray:

> *O dear God, I long to have a big soul, an honorable soul. Help me to live honorably with others and not blame and push away responsibility for my actions. Please give me the readiness to honestly face my true self. Guide my conviction to be authentic and let others know the real me. Show me how to be humble about my shortcomings and grow my trust in your plan. Amen.*

Breathing Deeper

1. In which moments of your life do you feel God's pleasure?
2. Taking responsibility for your actions is honorable. When is it tempting for you to blame others for your missteps?
3. You only need to make *one* small change at a time. What do you want to change right now? What is a first step you can take?

18

A Grounded Soul

"The soul was made to rest in God the way a tree rests in soil."
—John Ortberg

JOHN ORTBERG'S QUOTE GIVES ME a strong sense of peace. I picture a large long-established tree with roots splaying wide and branches full and vibrant. A tree resting in the soil is a picture of endurance and sturdy strength. It's not going anywhere; it can handle any storm that rages.

It also conjures up the idea of an old soul.

I would describe my friend Kathy as an old soul. She is secure in her place, honest and generous, fiercely loyal, and earnestly devoted to God. Her struggles are real, and she shares them without reluctance. What Kathy portrays on the outside matches who she is within. Her "tree" is deeply planted. Though storms may make it bow and sway, securely embedded roots hold her steady, and she does not break.

Because Kathy is a deep thinker, she helps me go deeper. She evokes new thoughts and broadens my mind with her insightful questions. Once, I was wrestling with whether faith and doubt could exist concurrently. Could a person claim to be a Christ-follower yet struggle with doubt? Our conversation led to her gentle response as she asked me if I thought having doubts was wrong; would God be displeased if I doubted? My first reaction was, "Yes! God wants me to believe and not doubt."

But her tender probing led me to study deeper and consider how many heroes in Scripture battled with doubt (think Moses, Abraham and Sarah, John the Baptist). Jesus never sent doubters away because they doubted. He continued to love them, reinforced the reasons for having faith, and encouraged them to keep searching. Kathy taught me to make room for doubt and to let God be a part of the journey toward stronger faith. I appreciated her kindness as she helped me think outside my realm, learning more sensitivity to the wider world, and seeing with clearer eyes.

Who in your life would you describe as "one well-planted, like a tree in soil?" What occurs in you when you spend time with this person? What do you learn? What are the qualities you see in them and how might you imitate them in your own life? How would those people respond if they were in your situation? It helps to picture yourself responding similarly.

Perhaps the person you admire is generally upbeat, joy filled, and can find the positive whatever their plight. How might you strive to react more like them, with gratitude for your circumstance? It takes only a small effort to adjust your responses.

Sure, you aren't always in a sublime state of mind, ready to imitate and grow, but keep making steps to adjust and ground yourself in good soil. As you do, you will be able to admit your faults more freely and acknowledge your strengths. Also remember, you have fine qualities that others will want to imitate. Examples go both ways.

See yourself as a pilgrim on this journey not as a perfect person who has already arrived.

Nurture Your Soul

Nurture (Latin: *nutrire*) means "to nourish, feed, or cherish." It speaks of cultivating, carefully tending, and tenderly training. Whether you cultivate a small plant, a small child, or a significant relationship, what you nurture matters; it carries weight today, tomorrow, and years from now.

So it goes with your soul, because what you focus on expands.

As you focus on nurturing your soul, soul health increases. Check in frequently on your soul's well-being and determine how you can adjust your focus. Rather than zeroing in on the troubles, could you modify your perspective and look for more helpful solutions?

Welcome any signals coming from your soul. Listen closely. What might it be telling you to focus on? Try not to ignore God's nudges; let him use whatever he can to nurture your soul. My preacher says, "If God taps you on the shoulder (by some comment you hear, a circumstance in your life or some thought passing through your mind), maybe he's saying to you, 'Hey, ask me about this. Pay attention to this.'"

Focus means *intentional* contemplation. Rob Reimer, author of *Soul Care*, a well-known book helping people find freedom and fullness in Christ, tells us, "Every time we pick up the Bible, we are one breath away from a fresh encounter with the Living God." A fresh encounter energizes and excites your soul. You may gain an insight you hadn't seen before or expand a long-held conviction. This fresh nourishment may deepen your faith or reawaken your heart. It could simply help you appreciate a meaningful moment with your Creator.[19]

Spark Your Soul

There has been a recent trend to declutter your home by choosing which of your possessions "spark joy." I have done some serious cleaning-out of drawers and closets and feel less encumbered by having less stuff. It's an incredible concept and is extremely good for the consumer in me.

I wonder if there is a parallel to the spiritual side of life? What clutter do we hold onto in our hearts that robs us of joy and needlessly weighs us down?

In Richard Walker's book *Twenty-Four Hours a Day*, he says, "Anyone can fight the battles of just one day. It is only when you and I add the battles of those two awful eternities, yesterday and tomorrow, that we break down."[20]

Two *awful* eternities. When you hang onto anguish about missteps of the past or wring your hands wondering what may happen in the days ahead, you will rob yourself of joy in the present. These are the eternities on either side of today.

My sister has made progress by living in what she calls "day tight" compartments. All she has is this one day, today, and nothing more. She places her focus here and strives not to worry about the future nor mourn the past. It doesn't mean to ignore the past or pay little attention to what is ahead, but instead, it means maintaining a focus on today even as you gaze out in both directions.

The words of Jesus point to this helpful mindset, "Look at the birds of the air; they do not sow or reap or store away in barns, and yet your heavenly Father feeds them. Are you not much more valuable than they? Can any one of you by worrying add a single hour to your life?" (Matthew 6:26-27).

Every life is full of unexpected twists and turns. The path to joy may not always be clear and straightforward, but rather than worrying and fretting about where the path leads, like those birds, let go of situations outside your control. Focus on what brings joy to your soul today.

Here are a few ideas that may spark your soul. When it does, sit up and acknowledge it as the spark it is, allow it to refresh you:

>Spotting a bluebird outside the window
>Looking up on a dark night and seeing trillions of stars, or only one
>A phone call with good news that lifts your heart
>You receive a commendation from your boss
>Walking on a beach and running your toes through the sand
>A mountain hike and hearing only the forest sounds
>A heart-to-heart talk with a friend
>Listening to music you enjoy
>An encouraging card in your mailbox
>Making homemade soup
>Seeing a photo of a loved one
>Calling someone who makes you smile
>Going back to school
>A hot cup of coffee this morning

Small as they are, such instances help us find joy. Think of it as a treasure hunt, seeking any gem you can find, and allow the moment to enhance your outlook and refresh your spirit. Remember, what you focus on expands; joy multiplies as we feed and nurture it.

It all works together to help beautify your soul! Certainly, every moment of every day will *not* be joy filled, but if you can center in on any small joy, it is like finding the X on a treasure map!

Remember, God wants to restore and ground you. Release the burdens from yesterday and the worries about tomorrow; focus on what you have today. Rest quietly, picture yourself as the tree in the soil, grounded and sturdy, and pray,

O my God, not everything in my life is as it should be but help me remember you make all things new. You bring sparks of joy to my days and lift my heart higher. As the light of your love spills over me, I feel it nourishing and grounding me. Plant me deeper with your gentle nudges and remind me of your role in my life. I will listen and respond. Amen.

Breathing Deeper

1. Who is an old soul in your life? What occurs in you when you spend time together?
2. How has God tapped you on the shoulder? Might he be saying, 'Hey, ask me about this. Pay closer attention here."
3. How are you carrying the "awful eternities" from yesterday and tomorrow? How can you choose to live in a "day tight" manner?

19

The Steadfast Soul

"A river cuts through rock not because of its power but because of its persistence."
—Jim Watkins

LAST YEAR I JOINED A local boot camp style exercise program to help me get stronger physically. It was pretty intimidating to join a class with many who were younger and faster. It had been a while since I'd been in a group workout, but I had to start somewhere.

I chose the 5:30 a.m. class, with the delusion that because it was still dark at that hour there would be fewer eyes to see my struggle. We ran up and down hills, lifted weights, and did push-ups, with me consistently being the last to finish the reps or cross the line. I felt foolish, and the temptation to quit was intense!

But three times each week I showed up.

After the workouts, I weakly staggered to the parking lot, barely able to open the car door. However, as the weeks passed, I was encouraged to notice small gains: I could do more push-ups and run faster!

What were the lessons learned?

- Keep showing up
- Don't give up because it is hard

- Repeat until you've mastered it (or at least until you don't have to hobble to your car like a wizened crone)

The same is true in developing your beautiful soul. It means you remain steadfast in your determination, and persistent in your effort to overcome any setback. Sometimes it helps to step out of your comfort zone no matter how awkward or difficult. Any decision to improve yourself will continually be thwarted, and there will be many chances to quit. But if you keep working, returning, and trying again, you will experience your soul filling with boundless joy and courage.

Thomas Edison is a historic example of a steadfast spirit. When a reporter asked him how he felt about failing two thousand times before harnessing electricity into the bulb, he responded, "I did not fail. I invented the light bulb. It was simply a two thousand-step process."

How many steps will it take you to build soul wellness? Like strengthening a muscle, you must train it consistently and keep pushing further. No one expects strength without a struggle. Progress comes when you hang on and keep working at it. To attain a beautiful soul means you work steadily through difficulty or disappointment and persevere. Even when storms rage.

The idea is to keep your eyes on your target. American philosopher Vernon Howard tells us: "The beam from a lighthouse is not affected by howling wind and rain, and it remains perfectly steadfast and unaffected by the storm." As storms come (and they will come), you keep your focus fixed like a beam casting across the roiling water. As you remain unswerving, you will see growth in your soul. You need to "let your eyes look straight ahead; fix your gaze directly before you. Give careful thought to the path at your feet and be steadfast in all your ways" (Proverbs 4:25-26). The soul heals not because there are no setbacks but because you remain resolute to the plans God has for your life. Keep "your eyes set straight ahead." Other versions of this verse add nuance:

"Don't even turn your head" (Living Bible).
"Keep your head up" (The Voice).
"Keep your eyes focused on what is right" (Expanded Bible).
"Look not asquint." (Old English Version). This one made me chuckle. If you want a clear visual, open your eyes wide! No squinting!

Keep your eyes on God even when you stumble, lose sight of your goal, or when your faith is shaken. Because he is steadfast, you can be too.

Anchor for the Soul

Any sailor understands there is a risk of being swept away by waves in a storm or drawn by unseen currents in the calm. An anchor is required to keep the ship steady and safe from drifting into dangerous waters. An anchor grounds and connects you to something bigger than yourself.

Gods' unchanging nature is the bedrock on which you can cast your anchor. The anchor holding your soul is hope in God. He will not disappoint you because the hope you gain from this connection comes not from a lack of storms but from the immovable rock that safely tethers you. "We have this hope as an anchor for the soul, firm and secure." (Hebrews 6:19). We need this anchor because:

- Difficulties are real.
  Sometimes they are mild, occasionally acute, but they are never easy. You will experience difficulties, but your soul will remain steady and secure when you are anchored to God, who never changes.
- Drifting is Real.
  Any vessel left on the water will drift if not anchored firmly and even water that appears calm is can be full of churning currents. What are the unseen currents under the surface of your life? How easy is it for you to ignore snags in your character stowed deep under the surface? No matter how long you've cared for your soul, you will tend to drift if you don't pay attention. It is in the nature of all things to drift, to fall into disrepair or chaos. This is why you must pay close attention and remain anchored to a strong foundation.
- Distraction is Real.
  It is easy to be lured into temporal pleasures and lose sight of the joy that comes from a close and consistent connection with God. Unless you firmly anchor your faith in him, you might settle for a fake imitation of soul health and miss out on the true gifts God has planned for your life.
- Disasters are real.
  There are forces that can drag the most powerful vessels off course, and as Mat Kearney sings in his song, "Closer to Love", all is takes is one phone call that can bring us to our knees. In any raging storm, having your anchor in God's foundation is desperately needed for your soul's survival.

Hope in the Rock holds your anchor secure. Also, there are trusted individuals who steady your boat and help you set your anchor.

A Kindred Soul

Who inspires you?

Who helps you make better choices and speaks truth to your soul? (It's fun to imagine their soul nodding toward ours in understanding or even rolling their eyes at our messed-up thinking. They know us too well!) Savor any soul connection with these individuals. Find ways to be with them and allow your hearts to be knit together.

An article I read suggested that rather than making New Year's resolutions this year, instead write the names of people you admire and would like to imitate, then focus on this as your goal. It led me to think about who I esteem and why, and which components of their souls speak loudest to me. It was a gratifying exercise because real-life examples are easier to follow than resolutions. One person is well read. I can imitate him and expand my knowledge; another is generous, an area in which I desire to grow. Another friend is incredibly steady in her faith. Her tangible example of managing hardships inspires me and shows me the way. One gal is such a prayer warrior. I long to be more like her!

Find ways to imitate people in your life who encourage, energize, and challenge you. They are put there by God to impact your soul.

People who influence you and those you influence; these are kindred souls. It is part of God's plan to use you to make an impression on each other's faith.

Consider now the Rock who anchors you and pray:

O unchanging God, I rest in the soothing thought that you remain faithful and steadfast. Help me cast my anchor on you and not the shifting sands or waves. Keep my eyes on you as the storms come and go. Thank you for the fellow souls you have put in my life to impact me and help me maintain a beautiful soul. Amen.

Breathing Deeper

1. Making the soul steadfast is like strengthening a muscle. What "spiritual" exercise can you incorporate into your life to develop a steadfast soul?
2. Difficulties, drifting, distraction and disasters are real forces that push you off track. What anchors your soul deeper with God? What more can you do?
3. Who are the people you admire and would like to imitate? Which components of their soul speak loudest to you?

20

True Beauty

"Lord, make me an instrument of your peace.
Where there is hatred, let me sow love.
Where there is injury, pardon.
Where there is faith, doubt.
Where there is despair, hope.
Where there is darkness, light.
Where there is sadness, joy."
—The Peace Prayer, Author unknown

THERE IS SUCH SIMPLICITY IN making the better choice. Life's challenges come at you fast; they can suffocate your efforts to do the right thing and quash your progress if you don't safeguard the priority of soul fitness.

Author Anne Lamott, determined to develop a more loving nature, told herself, "If you want to feel loving . . . do something loving." It's not a big, complicated idea. In the silence of your own soul, think about what you'd like to improve and how you might try this in your life. For example,

If you want meaningful friendships, give more of yourself.
If you long to be kinder, choose nicer words.
If you want more compassion, stand in the shoes of others.

If you hope for open-mindedness, connect with those different from you.
If you want soul health, do something healthful for your soul.

Imagine days, months, and years of making the better choice. Picture the positive strides you will accumulate as you stay in step with soul health.

Choose to Say Yes!

When Lindsay turned fifty, she committed the entire year to saying yes to whatever God placed before her. It inspired me to take on a similar mantle and challenge myself to say yes to whatever God brought across my path for one year. As I thought about this commitment, my eyes widened with panic as I considered what might be asked of me. I took a deep breath and said, "Yes!"

Once the decision was made it astounded me how frequently the word *yes* popped up. On a billboard, in Scripture, and on a notecard from a friend. I found examples of *yes* in books, on plaques at the gift shop, and in email newsletters. So many prompts came my way, it validated my decision.

I answered yes to learn how to paddleboard, build a new friendship, and join a local women's club. There were days I struggled to say yes—while completing daily pushups, accepting a challenging speaking engagement, and memorizing Scripture. It also became tangible in myriad little ways, like moving my desk to another room, painting a door seafoam blue, and getting bangs cut in my hair. The point of the undertaking was to open gates of possibility. What could God do with an open and ready vessel? What could he pour into me?

What might God do when you say yes?

You can say yes to upstanding behavior which allows your soul to flourish. God will strengthen you and help you make progress because it is in his heart to build you up. Listen to the hope of this psalmist: "On the day I called, you answered me; my strength of soul you increased" (Psalm 138:3, ESV).

It will take effort.

Make room for every emotion of the soul. They all combine to strengthen beauty within and make life wonderful. Don't simply wait until you feel like doing right or wait for your circumstances to be perfect before you act. There will always be thorny issues thrown your way, but with a yes, you can find a way through the brambles.

An ancient Greek axiom states, "No one ever steps into the same river twice, for it is not the same river, and you are not the same person." Every yes leads you to a new thought, a new approach, or a whole different direction. It is within the realm of possibility to make steps toward a beautiful soul.

The time is always *now*. So say yes to the right thing, *right now!*

God has given you a mind to comprehend and instilled in you a desire to grow and improve. Because you are open to it, your heart unfurls toward beauty in your soul. What you have learned about soul health has expanded your mind and has helped you make choices to engage your heart. Living with a beautiful soul lies wide open before you!

The Oak in the Acorn

A small acorn holds everything within it to become a mighty and massive oak. What a concept! The oak tree is already in the acorn. What if I told you the soul God placed in you is like an acorn, and God, the mighty Oak, is already in you? Though it may be hard to fathom, be aware God put this immense potential inside little you.

Take a few moments to absorb this staggering thought.

What is the purpose of this cherished gift? What will you do with it?

Thomas Aquinas wrote, "There is within every soul a thirst for happiness and meaning." Your meaning will become clear and your thirst for happiness quenched as you grow into the magnificent tree God planted. As you develop into the person he destined you to be, you will bear a better resemblance to your Creator, and your life will be the finger that points others to him.

Contrary to popular culture, your purpose is not to work for a life of ease and luxury or to try to feel good about your accomplishments. God created you to reflect *his love* and reveal him to others. Showing God to others through love is where meaning and thirst-quenching happens.

True beauty in your soul shows in how you carry yourself, how you treat others, and how you accept yourself, flaws and scars included. It is the light that pours out from you and is a grace that others can't help but feel.

Everyone you care about, every person for whom you are responsible, and anyone you meet will benefit when a beautiful, well-maintained "whole" you shows up. Persevere in soul health for your sake *and* for the sake of those you love.

A striking passage in the Old Testament exclaims, "[God] has made everything beautiful in its time. He has set eternity in the human heart; yet no one can fathom what God has done from beginning to end" (Ecclesiastes 3:11). God placed the compelling concept of eternity in your soul. He has imprinted on you a natural desire to seek him, know him, and be with him.

Though it may be tough to grasp, "The earth belongs to God. Everything in all the world is his!" (Psalm 24:1, TLB). This includes *you*. It encompasses your worries and all that confounds you. It includes every person, every tragedy, every joy, every cell in your body, every question, every test, every pound, and every ache. It includes sacred songs sung out of tune and every backward step.

And still, he longs to be with you now and for all eternity.

Pebbles in Your Pocket

A family took in a refugee mother and son when war came to their small village. When it was time to wash the boy's clothes, he insisted on keeping his trousers on. His mother, not understanding why, continued to press him. He finally put his hand in his pocket and pulled out two small stones. In tears, he told his mother that he had brought them from their village and feared they would be lost if taken from his pocket. The pebbles, he explained, were his connection to home; they represented his father and his grandfather who had stayed behind to fight. What a poignant reminder of the value of knowing where your home is.

What pebbles do you hold to help you remember "home?" You have picked up several morsels along this journey to a beautiful soul. Listed below are a few pebbles of truth you may be holding in your pocket:

- God created and planted your soul inside you; he meets you there in that place of quiet rest.
- God promises to restore your soul.
- By practicing natural rhythms of quiet and stillness, you can experience deeper self-awareness. Learn to

recognize the nudges from God, and remember the reasons soul health matters to you.
- A perfect soul is not the objective. Be intentional about your soul's condition. The door to spiritual growth opens wider the deeper you look into your injuries and scars. Wounds are inevitable, but they are not the end of your story!
- Transforming your soul is a life-long ambition—but well worth the effort. Aim for a big soul. Remember the divine nature of God; he is big enough to offer you every hope for recovery.
- A soul-filled life is not a solo journey. Being soul bound is worth the effort. You need others who also long for wholeness. And they need you.
- Being honorable, grounded, and steadfast in your soul helps you achieve your aim: a beautiful soul.

The more you hold onto these pebbles of wisdom, the more you will be able to heal, sustain and impact others, and find your path home. Oliver Wendell Holmes wrote, "The mind, once expanded to the dimensions of bigger ideas, never returns to its original size." Your eyes have been opened, and the door of your heart widened! In all of this, God is restoring you and making you beautiful. Persevere in soul health for your sake *and* for the sake of those you love.

Soul health matters. Just say yes as you pray these words:

O God, yes! Yes to beauty deep in my soul. Yes, to believing you have placed yourself in me as an oak in the acorn. Yes, to holding onto the thought of you in me as I go through my day. Yes, to believing the pebbles I hold in my hands are given to me by you. Help me to unswervingly lean into all things yes! Amen.

Breathing Deeper

1. "No one ever steps into the same river twice, for it is not the same river, and they are not the same person." How are you different each time you step into the "river"? How is the river different?
2. Why is it hard for you to fathom God, the mighty Oak, is already in you? What does it mean about the potential within you?
3. The earth and everything in it belongs to God. Since this includes you, how will you assimilate this thought into your daily walk with God?

Psst, You Have a Beautiful Soul!

"Wherever a beautiful soul has been there is a trail of beautiful memories."
—Ronald Reagan

THERE IS A FOLKTALE ABOUT an old woman who walks to the river each day to fill two buckets with water and carries them home on a bamboo pole laid across her stooped shoulders. One of the buckets is new and shiny; the other is worn and leaky. When she reaches her home, the shiny bucket is always full of water while the old one is only partially full.

One day, the leaky bucket apologized to the woman for not bringing home a full bucket of water. The woman smiled knowingly and looked back along the path and said to the old bucket, "Do you see all the lush flowers along the path I just walked? You have watered those for years and made my journey beautiful."

Whether you feel your soul is fresh and shiny or a bit leaky, God still treasures you and knows all that you offer. He sees you scatter beauty wherever you go. Your beautiful soul leaves a beautiful trail.

We set out at the beginning of the book to *dig deeper, talk truer,* and *look further ahead* to the dream of strengthening the soul. We have learned to slow and consider honest introspection. It is my deepest hope that you have found value in soul care, strength through personal reflection, and encouragement from those with whom your soul is bound.

As our time together comes to an end, press your shoulders back, sit tall, and draw in a long, deep breath. Then, with peace in your heart, exhale this heartfelt prayer:

O, great God, thank you for creating my rare and wonderful soul. I thank you for the mighty work you are doing to restore it. Thank you for healing my wounds, for transforming me, and making me beautiful.

Thank you for making me gold. Amen.

Acknowledgements

AS ANY WRITER KNOWS, YOU SPEND countless hours in solitude, banging away on the keyboard, mumbling to yourself, laughing out loud, and even shedding a few tears as you write. It can be an emotional experience to place yourself right there on the paper. This book could not have been completed without an array of supporters, urging and emboldening me to cross the finish line. To the myriad friends and family who have cared for my soul, stood by my side, read pieces of this manuscript, and allowed me to bounce my crazy ideas around, I say, "Thank You!"

THE PATIENT Tom Marks – an anchored soul. On my days of doubt and worry of whether I could complete this book, you encouraged and supported me, and gently offered fresh perspective. Only another writer, and of course those who live with them, truly understand the hours and days that consume a soul with such a project. You are a marvel, you are steady, you are upright. I could never do what I do without you. My soul dearly loves yours.

THE TALENTED Marty Stradley – a true soul. My wonderful and capable sister diligently scrubbed the entire manuscript clean of my meanderings and shone light onto unclear areas. Her gentle attention to detail and the big picture is nothing less than incredible. The help she has offered to me is inestimable, not only in this undertaking but truly in my whole life. She is one who possesses a beautiful soul.

THE AUTHENTIC Bonny Peterson – an honest soul. From my earliest memories, my younger sister has brought joy and kindness into my life. Her love is true and her devotion endless. I lean on her and she never fails to hold me up. She has an unassuming soul whom I trust with mine.

THE FAITHFUL Suzanne Baity – a devoted soul, who seems to know what I need each time we talk. Her calls always arrive at just the right moment and provide me with a swell of faith to carry on. Her soul and my soul are friends.

THE REFRESHER Renee Loheed – a joyful soul. Renee showed tremendous enthusiasm from the earliest days when the ideas were just forming about this book. Her comments on the early drafts boosted my confidence that there is a wide audience for this topic. Her belief in me refreshes my soul.

THE STEADY Kathyrn Hollister – a kind soul. Her wisdom pushed me to think outside my tiny sliver of the world and widen my view to this immense creation in which we live. Her faith helps me hold onto mine.

THE GENUINE Vicki Garrett – a tender soul. She reminds me to practice what I preach. Her authentic love for God strengthens mine.

THE CHEER SQUAD: To all who have stood solid on the sidelines, your input, support, and encouragement has helped me boundlessly.

ACKNOWLEDGEMENTS

- Thank you to my children, Jessica, Stephanie, and Ben, for your integral role in encouraging my own soul health. Our conversations revive me and lift my spirit. To my grandchildren, who refresh my soul over and over, I love you more today than I did yesterday!
- To those friends and relatives who have loved and shepherded my soul: Joyce Branson, Bonny Carter, Teri Cheney, Diane Durgin, the late Lucy Forney, Marita Forney, Kay McKean, Renee Sanchez, and Denise Schmitt. Thanks for asking about the book, thanks for your enthusiasm, and mostly thank you for your prayers. Your kindnesses helped me more than you can know.
- There are those in every city in which I've lived who have kept an eye on my soul. I cherish our memories and am convinced that my spiritual growth has been amplified by your support. Thank you for loving me.
- A special thanks goes to those who shared their expertise and added "flavor" to this book: Becky Moyer, for sharing her knowledge of the respiratory system; and to the late Lisa Selby, for her beautiful insight to music and the very vital rest notes.
- Thanks to the talented team at Illumify Publishing, especially to Karen Bouchard for her helpful advice as my writing coach. Always a joy to work together.

God, lastly, I thank you for your constant presence in my life. Thank you for leading me through every word and page of this book. You have helped me face the injuries to my own soul even when I was quaking with fear; and you opened up many roads of healing. Thank you for being the Lover of my soul, for restoring me, and for leading me. Yes, Lord, yes. Amen.

Notes

[1] Philip Yancey, *Reaching for the Invisible God* (Grand Rapids: Zondervan, 2002), 10.
[2] Dallas Willard, *Renovations of the Heart* (Colorado Springs: NavPress, 2002).
[3] Matthew Henry Bible Commentary, Romans 8:26, https://www.biblegateway.com/resources/matthew-henry/Rom.8.26-Rom.8.28.
[4] Sandra Thurman Caporale, from the Memorial Church of Christ in Houston, https://www.facebook.com/DioceseofReno/posts/7594074873965907?ref=embed_post.
[5] Marijohn Wilkin, "Scars in the Hands of Jesus," 1974.
[6] Yung Pueblo, *Lighter: Let Go of the Past, Connect with the Present, and Expand the Future* (New York: Harmony Books, 2022), 85.
[7] Ed Cyzewski, *A Christian Survival Guide* (Grand Rapids: Kregel Publications, 2014).
[8] Rachel Held-Evans, *Wholehearted Faith* (New York: HarperCollins, 2022), 166.
[9] Rachel Held Evans, *Wholehearted Faith* (New York: HarperOne, 2022), 166.
[10] Chris Germiel, *The Mindful Path to Self-Compassion: Freeing Yourself from Destructive Thoughts and Emotions* (New York: The Guilford Press, 2009), 2.
[11] Matthew Henry Bible Commentary, Job 26:7 (italics mine), https://www.biblegateway.com/resources/matthew-henry/Job.26.5-Job.26.14.
[12] Brené Brown, Gifts of Imperfection (Center City, Minn.: Hazelden, 2010), 53.
[13] Brown, *Gifts of Imperfection*, 11.
[14] Mark Manson, "The Hidden Costs of Happiness," Mark Manson website, https://markmanson.net/hidden-costs-of-happiness.
[15] K. J. Ramsey *The Book of Common Courage* (Grand Rapids: Zondervan, 2023).
[16] Oswald Chambers, *My Utmost for His Highest* (New York: Dodd, Mead & Co., 1935).
[17] Kate Bowler, *The Lives We Actually Have: 100 Blessings for Imperfect Days* (Colorado Springs: Convergent Books, 2023).
[18] Hugh Hudson, dir. *Chariots of Fire* (London: Enigma Productions, 1981).
[19] Rob Reimer, *Soul Care* (Franklin, Tenn.: Carpenter's Son Publishing, 2016).
[20] Richard Walker, *Twenty-Four Hours a Day* (Eastford, Conn.: Martino Fine Books, 2011).

Bible versions used:

All scripture quotations are from the NIV unless otherwise noted. Scripture quotations marked NET are from the NET Bible® copyright ©1996-2017 by Biblical Studies Press, L.L.C. http://netbible.com All rights reserved. Scripture quotations marked AMP are from The Amplified Bible Copyright © 2015 by The Lockman Foundation, La Habra, CA 90631. All rights reserved. Scripture quotations marked TPT are from The New Testament in Modern English by J.B Phillips copyright © 1960, 1972 J. B. Phillips. Administered by The Archbishops' Council of the Church of England. Used by Permission. Scripture quotations marked TPT are from The Passion Translation®. Copyright © 2017, 2018, 2020 by Passion & Fire Ministries, Inc. Used by permission. All rights reserved. ThePassionTranslation.com. Scripture marked ESV is from The Holy Bible, English Standard Version. ESV® Text Edition: 2016. Copyright © 2001 by Crossway Bibles, a publishing ministry of Good News Publishers. Scripture quotations marked MSG are from The Message Copyright © 1993, 2002, 2018 by Eugene H. Peterson Scripture quotations marked LSB are from the Legacy Standard Bible Copyright ©2021 by The Lockman Foundation. All rights reserved. Managed in partnership with Three Sixteen Publishing Inc. LSBible.org For Permission to Quote Information visit https://www.LSBible.org. Scripture quotations marked ISB are from The Holy Bible, International Children's Bible® Copyright© 1986, 1988, 1999, 2015 by Thomas Nelson. Used by permission. Scripture quotations marked NASB are from the New American Standard Bible®, Copyright © 1960, 1971, 1977, 1995, 2020 by The Lockman Foundation. All rights reserved. Scripture quotations marked VOICE are from The Voice Bible Copyright © 2012 Thomas Nelson, Inc. The Voice™ translation © 2012 Ecclesia Bible Society All rights reserved. Scripture quotations marked NLT are from the *Holy Bible*, New Living Translation, copyright © 1996, 2004, 2015 by Tyndale House Foundation. Used by permission of Tyndale House Publishers, Inc., Carol Stream, Illinois 60188. All rights reserved. Scripture quotations marked TLB are from The Living Bible copyright © 1971 by Tyndale House Foundation. Used by permission of Tyndale House Publishers Inc., Carol Stream, Illinois 60188. All rights reserved. Scripture quotations marked WEB are from the World English Version, public domain.

About the Author

JANET K. MARKS WRITES WITH unbridled optimism about the intriguing topic of soul health. She helps us find practical workarounds for difficult days and offers feasible options for a better frame of reference.

Woven into her writing are true stories, powerful insights, humor, and transparency about her own struggles to maintain a beautiful soul; she is a capable and compassionate guide. She invites others to embark with her on their own journey to a healthier soul.

When not writing books, blogs, and newsletters, she's out on speaking engagements, visiting family around the country, enjoying her vacation home in the Rockies, or digging in her burgeoning garden. She lives with her husband, Tom, just outside Dallas, Texas. They have three lovely children and three wonderful grandkids.

Visit her at *www.janetmarksauthor.com*

Janet is the author of *Three Little Decisions*: *How to Move Beyond the Bruises of Life.*

Life is full of decisions—little choices we rarely think about until something significant happens and shakes up the tedium of our day-to-day life. Some of these significant circumstances arrive not on a gentle breeze, which nudges us kindly along, but roars in like an arctic blast and blows us to the ground.

Several years ago, a strong blast hit my life; it knocked me sideways and landed me in a dark place. After too many days sitting in a pit of indignation and bitterness, it became clear: something had to change.

This was not how I wanted to live my life. Some kind of change was needed, but I felt uncertain how to proceed until a friend gave me a small gift that altered my outlook and helped me out of my pit.

Scan to purchase a copy today

Milton Keynes UK
Ingram Content Group UK Ltd.
UKHW012251291123
433483UK00006B/428